Praise for

Under the Broom Tree

B.E. Mathews deftly spins a wonderful and thought-provoking brief story that bridges the Old Testament with the modern day world, showing once again that the Bible and God's teachings transcend time and societal values. *Under the Broom Tree* will have you re-examine your faith and everything you thought to be true with insightful and delicious recountings of a woman coming to age in a culture that misplaces its values of what true beauty are.

—Julia Mathew, MSN

***

This book is for anyone who has ever felt lost, insecure, rejected or just plain tired. B.E. Matthews is raw and engaging, honestly sharing her own challenges and experiences by impactfully using the life of Elijah as a reference tool. She reminds us that when we feel dejected, divine comfort is always available by seeking God as our first source of refuge. She shows us how much we can accomplish if we search for blessings in the midst of our greatest trials and how much we can grow if we treat our "thorns" as gifts. Whether you are on top of a mountain, or in a deep valley, this book is for you!

—S.P. Spengler, ESQ

This compelling parallel between the lives of the author and Elijah makes an intriguing reference for anyone experiencing the trials of life. Far more than a testimonial, *Under the Broom Tree* is full transparency. It cuts to the heart of the matters: insecurity, rejection, and loss. Down to earth. Written for the ordinary person.

As a Christian, I personally recommend this book as a reminder that we all, like Elijah, struggle with the issues of life.

As a counseling professional, I recommend this book as a reference for overcoming adversities in life.

—Dora B. Mays, Ph.D.
Founder/CEO and Practitioner, AMaysing Services, Inc.

***

I have known Dr. Beena Mathews for several years. She is a fairly private person, more concerned with knowing the stories of others than in having her own known. So, in reading her book, I was both surprised and inspired by the stories she shared. As I was reading, I found myself repeatedly valuing the courage and vulnerability Dr. Mathews displays in her writing.

I wholeheartedly recommend her book to you, not because it will necessarily make you feel good, but because I believe it will make you more aware. For those who find themselves "under the broom tree," you will be more aware of God's love, care, and provision for you. For those who are not in such a season, I hope this book will help you be more aware of the those who are, the struggles they often silently face, and that it will motivate all of us to be more empathetic and supportive.

—Rev. Bruce Blagg
Pastor, President & Co-founder
Phoenix Advantage, Inc.

***

I have always enjoyed reading about Elijah, the prophet whose account in the Bible begins in I Kings 17 and ends in the Gospels when he, with Moses, appears with Jesus in the glorious splendor of the Transfiguration. To date, how many women's ministry events have I attended, small group Bible studies have I led, or even my own private quiet times where the focus had been on Elijah calling down fire from Heaven? Countless. So, when Beena sent me *Under the Broom Tree*, her own interpretation of the life and times of Elijah, I was intrigued.

With Elijah, we think about the prophet who prayed, and the rain stopped for three years in Israel. And he prayed once more, and oil filled the empty jugs of a widow in Zarephath. And he prayed again, and fire came down from Heaven at Mt. Carmel. But never do we start his story with, *"exhausted and weary, Elijah laid himself down under the broom tree and prepared to die."*

But Beena does. And she also reminds us, *God didn't scold Elijah but took care of his every need.*

What brings you under the broom tree, Beena asks? What pushes you to that place where you've not only forgotten all the things that God has done for you, but you feel completely overlooked by Him? That's where this story begins.

I love this perspective as much as I love this author. Friends for over a decade, Beena and I served in the children's ministry at our church, myself as the director and Beena, one of my most faithful leaders. We didn't know it at the time, but the children's lobby where we welcomed families every Sunday, whole and broken, was a broom tree. Beena and I shared a decade's worth of life-on-life under that broom tree with countless families, joyful and full, trodden, and brokenhearted. And as with Elijah, God didn't scold any of them but took care of their every need. That lobby was our own broom tree, too. Beena and I, runners. Mothers to sons. Professional women. Beena, a pediatrician and myself, an educator. We shared our very hearts with one another under the broom tree.

That's what I love about Beena's perspective on Elijah. God allowed us to see this great man in pain, in a defeated position, but cared for by a loving God.

Reader, go to your personal broom tree and see Elijah through Beena's eyes. You will not be disappointed as she weaves her personal stories into Elijah's, aligning with the events of the prophet's life. Thank you, Beena, for entrusting me with this beautiful story. Thank you most of all for starting with the broom tree.

—Jennifer King, PhD

UNDER THE
**BROOM
TREE**

B. E. MATHEWS

Published by KHARIS PUBLISHING, an imprint of
KHARIS MEDIA LLC.

Copyright © 2023 B. E. Mathews

ISBN-13: 978-1-63746-212-6

ISBN-10: 1-63746-212-3

Library of Congress Control Number: 2023935628

All KHARIS PUBLISHING products are available at
special quantity discounts for bulk purchase for sales
promotions, premiums, fund-raising, and educational
needs. For details, contact:
Kharis Media LLC
Tel: 1-630-909-3405
support@kharispublishing.com
www.kharispublishing.com

Dedication

Dedicated to my sons, Daniel and Jonathan.

Disclaimer

The opinions and beliefs presented in this book are solely those of the author and do not represent the ideas, beliefs, or opinions of any company or association with which the author has employment or affiliation.

Table of Contents

INTRODUCTION

I ts description is plain and unremarkable. It's an ordinary tree.

Trunk, branches, leaves.

Merriam-Webster's dictionary has two definitions for the broom tree. The first is "a shrub (*Baccharis scoparia*)," and the second is "a yellow-flowered prickly shrub (*Genista anglica*) found on the moors of northern Europe and England. *Encyclopedia Britannica* says of the broom tree, "It can be deciduous or evergreen" and usually has "compound leaves with three leaflets." It stands anywhere from three to ten feet tall.

It's not even exclusively found in one place in the world. There's nothing significant about the broom tree's beauty or height or location or its flowers.

But under a particular broom tree near Beersheba in Judah a remarkable interaction between God and man transpired. One of the greatest prophets of the Old Testament came to a full stop there and asked God to let him die. He was exhausted. He'd been running for his life and had come to the end of himself, to the limits of his own strength. He'd lost his will to continue living.

He hadn't been defeated by any foe. He hadn't suffered a loss. Quite the opposite.

He did this after a great victory, one of the grandest displays of God's Holy power recorded in the Bible, a book that's already packed with unimaginable, miraculous feats. And God had used this man to perform this supernatural marvel, this same man who slumped there, tapped out and broken.

He should have felt invincible.

And God could have scolded him and given him a heavy reprimand to remind him of everything He'd done through him, but God didn't do that. He let this weary man rest, and He cared for him where he laid himself down under the broom tree.

This esteemed man of God performed great miracles during his time and received his power from God through prayer. He prayed earnestly. James 5:16 (NIV) says, "The prayer of a righteous person is powerful and effective," and this tired man lived that out. People mistook Jesus for him, and they thought John the Baptist came in his spirit and power. This man of miracles embodied Acts 17:28 (NKJV) where it says, "For in Him we live and move and have our being." He joined Jesus at the Transfiguration, along with Moses, and where Moses represented the law, he represented the prophets.

This mighty individual never died but was instead taken up into heaven in what is described magnificently as a whirlwind of fire. The only other person in the Bible to be taken up to heaven without dying was Enoch in Genesis 5:24 (NIV) where it simply states, "Enoch walked faithfully with God; then he was no more, because God took him away." Yet God allows us to see this great man in pain, in a defeated position.

Why would God want us to see someone gifted with such extraordinary power in his weakness?

Because God wants us to see this person's humanity and how He loved him in his highs and his lows, in his triumph and in his despondency. God embraced him fully, and that is how He loves and embraces us.

AΩ

If the wealthy or the powerful or the beautiful were exempt from pain, then no Hollywood celebrity or famous musician in history would have ever attempted suicide. The pharmaceutical companies that produce SSRIs and anxiolytics would have significantly lower profit margins if it were not for this common thread in our human nature, and it's becoming more prevalent with younger people.

There's a generation of children affected by anxiety and depression and attempting to end their lives. There is still a stigma associated with mental illness. It's a tragedy that so many people are afraid to confront and deal with it in a healthy way.

Grief and heartache have never discriminated by wealth, or caste, or color, or gender, and they didn't in the Bible either. We've got great company there.

David, who was described as "a man after God's own heart" says,

"My life is consumed by anguish
and my years by groaning;
my strength fails because of my affliction,
and my bones grow weak" (Psalm 31:10, NIV).

Job, who was described as a righteous man, "blameless and upright," says, "Terrors overwhelm me; my dignity is driven away as by the wind, my safety vanishes like a cloud. And now my life ebbs away; days of suffering grip me. Night pierces my bones; my gnawing bones never rest" (Job 30:15-17, NIV).

Jesus in Gethsemane's garden is described this way, "…He began to be sorrowful and deeply distressed." Looking more like Adam than ever before, He shares with His friends, "My soul is exceedingly sorrowful even to death" (Matthew 26:37-38, NKJV).

What brings you under the broom tree? What pushes you to that place where you've not only forgotten all the things God has done for you, but you've felt completely overlooked by Him? Are we wrong to go there? Is it a bad place to be, or is it the place where you finally surrender yourself and let God sustain you?

We are more like this prophet among prophets than we realize. There are moments in life that bring us to the same place, to the same end of ourselves, where we utterly fail in our Plan A and must lay down every proceeding Plan, B through Z. Our pride is stripped. We're painfully aware of our frailty and shortcomings, and that's the place where God lets us rest, meets our needs, and strengthens us back to our feet.

I've been there under the broom tree. The first time I heard this man's story, I saw myself in him. I'd never performed a miracle but had tasted some success in my life. I'd seen God's blessings, but I so often chose to go my own way and took control, foolishly believing I actually had it. I forgot what it meant to be desperately in need of my Savior, and it always led me to a dark place. Then God showed up. He had, and still has, a way of meeting me at my lowest points, sustaining me, teaching me. Then He finally pressed upon me to share these experiences.

If my Savior Jesus Christ can hang naked and exposed on a cross to set you, me, and the world free, then I can bare my own soul if it sets just one person free from their pain. If I can reach one person with my transparency, show them they're not alone and that they've got a comrade shouldered up with them, then this endeavor is worth it.

So first, let's dive into the story of this great prophet.

Let's get acquainted with this miracle-worker who was described as being just like us.

Let's meet Elijah, the ordinary man.

Chapter One

OUR FRIEND, ELIJAH, THE ORDINARY MAN

"Elijah was a human being, even as we are…" James 5:17 (NIV).

He was an ordinary man with the same passions and emotions as us, but he prayed powerful prayers.

"The effective, fervent prayer of a righteous man avails much. Elijah was a man with a nature like ours and he prayed earnestly that it would not rain; and it did not rain on the land for three years and six months" (James 5:16-17, NKJV). Elijah's prayers had the power to control the weather.

He was the first person in the Bible to raise someone from the dead, but there's no book in the Bible titled after him.

He never died, but instead was taken by "a chariot of fire and horses of fire" up to heaven "in a whirlwind" (2 Kings 2:11, NIV).

But Elijah was introduced plainly and simply in 1 Kings as "Elijah the Tishbite, from Tishbe in Gilead" (1 Kings 17:1, NIV). We're told nothing about his background, lineage, or childhood. There's nothing interesting or noteworthy about the Tishbites or their history.

"Now Elijah the Tishbite, from Tishbe in Gilead, said to Ahab, 'As the Lord, the God of Israel, lives, whom I serve, there will be neither dew nor rain in the next few years except at my word'" (1 Kings 17:1, NIV). And it was so. Because Elijah prayed it, God stopped the rain from falling for three and a half years.

Who was Ahab, and why did Elijah pray for a drought to occur?

It was because Israel was the chosen nation of the one holy God, Jehovah, and she had forgotten Him and gone into such a destructive spiritual decline, especially under King Ahab. God used Elijah to call her back.

We need to understand how this situation came about in Israel. King David reigned for forty years, from 1010 through 970 BC and was considered the greatest of Israel's kings. Under him, the nation of Israel, made up of twelve tribes, was united and flourished, and some say that was when she was at her most powerful and influential in the ancient world. Solomon, David's son, succeeded him and was renowned for his wisdom. He's credited with building God's first holy temple in Jerusalem and was a brilliant author like his father. The nation prospered under him, but Solomon was influenced by his numerous foreign wives and went after other gods.

Things really changed for Israel after Solomon's death in 931 BC. His son Rehoboam inherited the throne, but subsequently, due to economic grievances, the twelve tribes of Israel became divided. Ten of the tribes, led by Jereboam I, who had been one of Solomon's officials, seceded and formed the Northern Kingdom.

The Southern Kingdom worshipped Jehovah or Yahweh, but Jereboam I introduced idolatry to the North. Ahab was the seventh king for the Northern Kingdom after Solomon's reign. The six before him, including Jereboam I, were all wicked. They led Israel into spiritual depravity. One of them killed his own father to take the throne and then annihilated his entire family. Another one committed suicide by burning himself alive.

Ahab was called the worst of all the six kings before him, and he received special mention in that he "did more evil in the eyes of the Lord than any of those before him" (1 Kings 16:30, NIV). He married Jezebel, a foreign princess from Phoenicia, who influenced him to push the worship of Baal into Israel.

Baal was considered a fertility deity and a god of rain and seasons who was symbolized by a bull or ram's head on a man's body. He was believed to have been married to a female deity named Asherah, goddess of fertility. Baal worship included sacred prostitution and the performance of rituals and magic, none of which were found in the worship of Jehovah. It was thought that sexual acts by both male and female prostitutes at Baal's temple would arouse Baal to make him bring rain so the land would be more fertile. Asherah was worshiped near trees and poles, hence in Scripture, the terms "Asherah poles" and "high places" denoted places of worship for these deities.

Child sacrifice was also an aspect of their worship. "They have also built the high places of Baal, to burn their sons with fire for burnt offerings to Baal" (Jeremiah 19:5, NKJV). In Deuteronomy 12:31 (NKJV) it says, "You shall not worship the Lord your God in that way; for every abomination to the Lord which He hates they have done to their gods; for they burn even their sons and daughters in the fire to their gods." In the location of the ancient city of Carthage (the Carthaginians were Phoenicians), there's archeological evidence of "Tophets," or places of child sacrifice, where the remains of infants and children were found in urns.[1]

God decided enough was enough, and He called Elijah out onto the scene. We don't know why God chose him or how. There's no account of his calling like there was with Moses at the burning bush on Mount Horeb or with young Samuel when he was lying down to sleep. The drought and famine caused by the prayer of

Elijah, a man whose name meant "my God is Yahweh," was an affront to people who were caught up in worshipping a false god of rain and fertile lands.

The scene between Elijah and the king occurred sometime during 874 through 853 BC. Elijah prayed for this economically devastating drought when Israel was under the reign of King Ahab and Queen Jezebel, the evilest of couples. This ordinary man essentially showed up from nowhere, confronted the ruler of his country, and gave a binding oath. He proclaimed his God as the one true God of Israel and declared that he was speaking on God's behalf. With confidence, he told the most powerful person in his nation that it wouldn't rain until he, Elijah, said the word.

One can imagine King Ahab's response. He had the option of feeling convicted, seeking mercy, and turning from idolatry, but he didn't. I suspect he didn't take this nobody from nowhere seriously until the drought happened. Once it did, our friend Elijah had to flee and hide.

"Then the word of the Lord came to Elijah: 'Leave here, turn eastward and hide in the Kerith Ravine, east of the Jordan. You will drink from the brook, and I have directed the ravens to supply you with food there. So he did what the Lord had told him. He went to the Kerith Ravine, east of the Jordan, and stayed there. The ravens brought him bread and meat in the evening, and he drank from the brook'" (1 Kings 17:2-6, NIV).

A "ravine" is a deep, narrow gorge with steep sides or a small, steep-sided narrow valley. It's typically worn down by a stream. The Kerith Ravine is still present today, south of the Sea of Galilee and north of where Elijah was originally from, Tishbe. Elijah took the next step God asked him to take. It was not only for his protection, but also to grow his trust and reliance on God.

We don't know how long he was there, but we have an idea of what he learned from God there. He must have learned how to rely on God for his daily bread. Ravens were intelligent birds, and here God showed His power over nature by instructing them to bring Elijah food. I imagine they brought him bread, vegetables and other crops they found while flying, and it was just enough for the meal for that day. Elijah witnessed God's faithfulness firsthand, and his very life depended on it. I imagine he kept praying earnestly for the drought to continue. Just like for many of us when we're stripped of comfort and company, this time alone for Elijah was when he really got to know God.

Eventually, the brook dried up because there was no rain. The drought that Elijah prayed for was affecting him directly. Generally, the human body can only survive without water for about three days. So God gave Elijah his next step. God sent him to a widow in Zarephath, which was where Jezebel was from in Phoenicia. Her father had been the priest-king of Tyre and Sidon. So Elijah trekked roughly eighty-five miles right into the territory of his enemies.

"Then the word of the Lord came to him: 'Go at once to Zarephath in the region of Sidon and stay there. I have directed a widow there to supply you with food.' So he went to Zarephath. When he came to the town gate, a widow was there gathering sticks. He called to her and asked, 'Would you bring me a little water in a jar so I may have a drink?' As she was going to get it, he called, 'And bring me, please, a piece of bread'" (1 Kings 17:8-11, NIV).

I don't know how Elijah knew which widow was the one God would direct to help him. It seems he fielded the first question to scope out the situation. He asked her for water. Remember there was a drought, so the fact that she turned to go get it probably encouraged him to request bread.

I'm not sure how God directed the widow. Perhaps it was a nudging in her heart that compelled her to help this stranger when her own cupboards were bare. Her first words to him were, "'As surely as the Lord your God lives,' she replied, 'I don't have any bread – only a handful of flour in a jar and a little olive oil in a jug. I am gathering a few sticks to take home and make a meal for myself and my son, that we may eat it – and die'" (I Kings 17:12, NIV). Her situation was bleak, and her hesitation was understandable. She had a child at home to consider as well, not just herself. She also said, "the Lord *your* God," which suggests to me that she wasn't necessarily a believer in Jehovah and was likely a Gentile.

Elijah told her to not be afraid. It's significant he said that to her, and we'll discuss more about it later. "Elijah said to her, "'Don't be afraid. Go home and do as you have said. But first make a small loaf of bread for me from what you have and bring it to me, and then make something for yourself and your son'" (1 Kings 17:13, NIV). Then he made her an audacious, faith-filled oath. He promised her that her food wouldn't run out. "For this is what the Lord, the God of Israel, says: 'The jar of flour will not be used up and the jug of oil will not run dry until the day the Lord sends rain on the land'" (1 Kings 17:14, NIV).

What God promised the widow through Elijah came true. "She went away and did as Elijah had told her. So there was food every day for Elijah and for the woman and her family. For the jar of flour was not used up and the jug of oil did not run dry, in keeping with the word of the Lord spoken by Elijah" (1 Kings 17:15-16, NIV).

Now that sounds like another extraordinary display of God's daily provision. There was just enough for the day; they weren't baking loaves for the week. It's like how God tried to teach the wandering Israelites in the desert to rely on Him for their daily bread, the manna in the morning.

Elijah sounded like someone with dynamic and effective prayers. Do we still think we're like him? At this point in his story, I found it difficult to relate to him, and it wasn't even the most incredible thing he did. He was just getting started.

Chapter Two

AN ORDINARY MAN RAISES THE DEAD

After some time had passed, while Elijah was still staying with her, this same widow's son became ill, worsened, and died. "She said to Elijah, 'What do you have against me, man of God? Did you come to remind me of my sin and kill my son?'" (1 Kings 17:18, NIV).

I'm not sure what sin she was talking about. It sounds like there was something on her conscience weighing upon her, and she believed God was now punishing her by taking her son's life. She blamed Elijah since he was God's man. She'd likely developed a sense of security having Elijah there with this flour and oil that didn't run out, but now she felt let down in a major way. Any hope she had in a future vanished when life's breath left her son. She had no husband to take care of her. Having sons myself, I can only imagine the depth of her pain.

Elijah's response was immediate, but this same man who told the widow to not be afraid now sounded like he was. He didn't make any retaliatory comment back at her or make any attempt to comfort her. He'd been living in her home, so we can assume he knew the boy and had interacted with him, too. He probably saw through her harsh words to their core, to her overwhelming grief, and maybe he felt some of the same.

It doesn't sound like Elijah was prepared for this. God didn't warn him. Have you ever been diligent in your prayer life, felt like you were doing pretty good in your habits and in your thought life, and suddenly something negative and unexpected happened that pulled the rug out from under you? I have, and the first thought that popped into my head was, "Why God?" I negotiated with Him that I was living right and didn't deserve a bad thing to happen. I reviewed my recent behavior and tried to find some fault of mine for which I was being punished, some slight I'd committed against God.

The world is a fallen place. We're not necessarily being punished. We're promised to have difficulty, to have pain, to experience loss. In John 16:33 (NIV), Jesus says, "… in this world you will have trouble…"

But don't leave it there. Finish that verse. "… but take heart! I have overcome the world." That's another promise. Don't lean away from Him when trouble comes. Do the opposite and lean in because that's how you'll get through it. Frank Peretti in *No More Bullies: For Those Who Wound or Are Wounded* wrote, "God does not waste an ounce of our pain or a drop of our tears; suffering doesn't come our way for no reason, and He seems efficient at using what we endure to mold character. If we are malleable, He takes our bumps and bruises and shapes them into something beautiful."[2]

"'Give me your son,' Elijah replied. He took him from her arms, carried him to the upper room where he was staying, and laid him on his bed. Then he cried out to the Lord, 'Lord my God, have you brought tragedy even on this widow I am staying with, by causing her son to die?'" (1 Kings 17:19-20, NIV).

I've gained some information from these verses. First of all, the widow's son was probably not a grown man; he was just a boy. Elijah was physically able to take him from the widow's arms and carry him to an upper room. I have four sons. The older two are my stepsons, and the younger two I birthed. If one of them became ill and died, I believe my first thought would be that God was punishing me for something I did wrong, some grave misstep of my own. As a mom, losing a child is worse than myself dying. I would rather die in place of one of them, and if I could make some cosmic exchange I would.

Elijah says something interesting about tragedy being brought even on this widow. It sounds like someone he knew personally or with whom he had stayed before suffered a tragedy. Maybe he even felt somewhat responsible for whatever sorrow they experienced, or maybe he knew it was his words that shut the heavens and stopped the rainfall. He saw the suffering of people around him from the drought, and he felt like this widow was suffering even more because he was there in her home. Elijah doesn't give her any answer as to why this happened to her son or assure her that it was to reveal God's glory. He doesn't reassure her in any way that he wasn't the cause of the tragedy or that he would be able to help the boy. There's no "fear not" or "wait and see what God will do" for her from him.

Elijah doesn't stop at the widow's questioning of him or at his own questioning to God. He prays for the boy to be healed in an unconventional way. "Then he stretched himself out on the boy three times and cried out to the Lord, 'Lord my God, let this boy's life return to him!'" (1 Kings 17:21, NIV). People don't usually stretch themselves out and lay on top of someone's child like this. Nowadays it would be considered weird behavior and would probably prompt someone to call the authorities. He was asking God to raise this child from the dead, to resurrect him, something that should have been impossible. It had never been done before in the Bible. His prayer was fervent, and it sounded as if he was trying to impart his own vitality and breath into the child. Elijah's first instinct was to pray. It was the first resort for him, not the last. It should be first for us, too.

Notice before Elijah asked God to bring the boy back to life, he cried out to God and questioned Him, and this is completely okay to do. How many times in the Psalms did David put all his feelings out before God? He poured out his pain. We don't have to be politically correct with God. We should be respectful, but we should also be open and honest. Nothing is hidden from His sight, but there is something that moves the heart of Almighty God when we willingly share ourselves with Him and lay our souls bare.

Elijah didn't stop when his request failed the first time or when it failed the second time. He executed the same tactic three times. In the Bible, the number three was sacred. There's the Holy Trinity – Father, Son and Holy Spirit, and the third day was when Jesus rose from the dead. Perhaps there's a lesson there for us. If you haven't tried earnestly at least three times, then you haven't tried at all.

"The Lord heard Elijah's cry, and the boy's life returned to him, and he lived. Elijah picked up the child and carried him down from the room into the house. He gave him to his mother and said, 'Look, your son is alive!' Then the woman said to Elijah, 'Now I know that you are a man of God and that the word of the Lord from your mouth is the truth'" (1 Kings 17:22-24, NIV).

Now she's a believer. Apparently, the never-ending oil and flour weren't proof enough of God's power for this widow. What all do we have to go through before we finally believe? Are the tragedies we endure actually conduits for God to forcefully infuse His miracle-working love into our lives so we will believe Him to be who He is? Imagine for Elijah how this strengthened his faith. He'd probably never heard of anyone coming back from the dead, much less having a hand in it.

Jesus, being the only begotten Son of God, understood the significance of "the only." In fact, there are just three instances in the New Testament where we read about Jesus resurrecting someone from death. He most likely did more than that, but God gave us details on these three: his friend Lazarus (Mary and Martha's only brother), the daughter of Jairus (his only child), and the son of the widow at the gates of Nain (her only son).

It was the faith of Elijah that raised the first person in the Bible from the dead. Abraham, Moses, Isaac, Jacob and Joseph – none of them did it, and we have yet to get into his most extraordinary feat. However, after Elijah did the next impossible miracle, he ran for his life, suddenly terrified. How was it possible for a man to be so afraid when he had access to supernatural power?

It's because he was still just an ordinary person, like us.

Chapter Three

ELIJAH, THE FIRESTARTER

The Bible chronicles the reigns of Israel's kings in the books of 1 and 2 Kings, and most of them get only part of a chapter, however, King Ahab gets six chapters. This is not because he's such a great king, but because his story is Elijah's story.

Elijah was the enemy of Ahab and Jezebel, and he was number one on their most wanted list. Up until this time, God kept him hidden and sustained him. Then in that third year, God instructed Elijah to come out of hiding, "'Go and present yourself to Ahab, and I will send rain on the land'" (1 Kings 18:1, NIV).

Elijah obeyed, though I can't imagine how hard that must have been for him. I think he was emotionally torn. He probably felt some relief that it was finally time to move from his season of waiting, but the move God required of him likely had him shaking in his sandals. Nonetheless, Elijah moved because it was God's command. He didn't pull a Jonah and try to run away; he went to his Nineveh instead.

Elijah presented himself to a Jewish man named Obadiah who believed in Yahweh and worked in a position of authority and trust in King Ahab's palace. Obadiah revealed to Elijah, "'As surely as the Lord your God lives, there is not a nation or kingdom where my master has not sent someone to look for you. And whenever a nation or kingdom claimed you were not there, he made them swear they could not find you. But now you tell me to go to my master and say, 'Elijah is here.' I don't know where the Spirit of the Lord may carry you when I leave you. If I go and tell Ahab and he doesn't find you, he will kill me. Yet I your servant have worshiped the Lord since my youth. Haven't you heard, my lord, what I did while Jezebel was killing the prophets of the Lord? I hid a hundred of the Lord's prophets in two caves, fifty in each, and supplied them with food and water. And now you tell me to go to my master and say, 'Elijah is here.' He will kill me!'" (1Kings 18:10-14, NIV). Elijah assured him that he would meet Ahab that very day. Obadiah conveyed the message to Ahab, and they met at a designated place. When Ahab saw Elijah, he addressed him, "'Is that you, you troubler of Israel?'" (I Kings 18:17, NIV). Unlike their first meeting, this time, Elijah had Ahab's attention and wary respect.

Elijah snapped back. "'I have not made trouble for Israel,' Elijah replied. 'But you and your father's family have. You have abandoned the Lord's commands and have followed the Baals. Now summon the people from all over Israel to meet me on Mount Carmel. And bring the four hundred and fifty prophets of Baal and the four hundred prophets of Asherah, who eat at Jezebel's table'" (1 Kings 18:18-19, NIV).

Elijah called for a standoff, one man against four hundred and fifty, God's prophet against the false prophets, and on a mountaintop no less. He wanted all of Israel to gather and witness. Mount Carmel was on the border of Israel and Phoenicia (Jezebel's home) and was the highest point in that area, roughly 1800 feet above sea level. I imagine word spread about this faceoff, and the people gathered over a period of days. They probably camped out and talked amongst one another, anticipating what exciting show would unfold. I suspect they were also hoping for it to finally rain, for the drought to end.

Picture if you will, a proud, lofty king with a gang of four hundred and fifty on one side and on the other side, just one man. And then there's the crowd watching with palpable expectation.

The first thing Elijah did was call the people out on their sin. "And Elijah came to all the people, and said, 'How long will you falter between two opinions? If the Lord is God, follow Him; but if Baal, follow him'" (1 Kings 18:21, NKJV).

The people had no response. They wouldn't choose one or the other, neither option A nor B. God would not allow both, which is probably the option C they wanted. It's the same for us. God doesn't want us on the fence, living like the world lives and having some Christian habits. He wants us to clearly decide so when we choose Him, the life we live makes it obvious and evident to anyone who knows us that we are His people.

Since they were speechless, Elijah proposed a competition. They would each offer a sacrifice. Baal's prophets would call on him, and Elijah would call on Jehovah. Whoever answered first by lighting the fire was the winner.

It was a sudden death match, and Elijah let the opposition go first. If they won, the contest was over, and Elijah would lose. It didn't seem like a wise strategy to allow his opponent to take the first shot. This showed Elijah's absolute confidence in Jehovah. He knew the enemy was defeated. For Elijah, the outcome was already set. He allowed the prophets of Baal to go first for the benefit of the Israelites who were watching.

He let them choose the bull they wanted to sacrifice. "Then Elijah said to the people, 'I alone am left a prophet of the Lord, but Baal's prophets are four hundred and fifty men. Therefore let them give us two bulls; and let them choose one bull for themselves, cut it in pieces, and lay it on the wood, but put no fire under it; and I will prepare the other bull, and lay it under the wood but put no fire under it. Then you call on the name of your gods, and I will call on the name of the Lord; and the God who answers by fire, he is

God.' So all the people answered and said, 'It is well spoken'" (1 Kings 18:22-24, NKJV).

The people agreed to this contest. Now Elijah specifically said for no fire to be under the wood. Baal's prophets would sometimes hide a small flame under their sacrifices and fan it into a blaze to make it look like Baal had created the fire. It was one of the ways they fooled the masses.

So Baal's prophets got to it. They called out to him for hours. "So they took the bull which was given them, and they prepared it, and called on the name of Baal from morning till noon, saying, 'O Baal, hear us!' But there was no voice; no one answered. Then they leaped about the altar which they had made" (1 Kings 18:26, NKJV).

At noon, Elijah decided to have some fun. He was sarcastic with them and started talking smack. He said, "'Cry aloud, for he is a god; either he is meditating, or he is busy, or he is on a journey, or perhaps he is sleeping and must be awakened'" (1 Kings 18:27, NKJV). The term "busy" here implied that he was using the bathroom.

The prophets of Baal upped their performance. "So they cried aloud, and cut themselves, as was their custom, with knives and lances, until blood gushed out on them. And when midday was past, they prophesied until the time of the offering of the evening sacrifice" (1 Kings 18:28-29, NKJV).

What do you think happened next? Right, nothing, dead silence, so "no voice, no one answered, no one paid attention" (1 Kings 18:29, NKJV). It was not an "aha!" moment for Ahab. No doubt he was embarrassed and cranky with his gods, who were clearly doomed to fail from the start. Jehovah was the only God. Elijah knew it, and he needed to remind the flock of "lost sheep" observers of that fact.

"Then Elijah said to all the people, 'Come near to me.' So all the people came near to him. And he repaired the altar of the Lord that was broken down. And Elijah took twelve stones, according to the number of tribes of the sons of Jacob, to whom the word of the Lord had come, saying, 'Israel shall be your name'" (1 Kings 18:30-31, NKJV).

Elijah took the time to gather the twelve stones representing the twelve original tribes of Israel. The people needed to remember who they were and whose they were. After all the drama, dancing, cutting and bleeding spectacle they'd witnessed, he drew them close and reminded them of what was really important and how it was supposed to have been. "Then with the stones he built an altar in the name of the Lord; and he made a trench around the altar large enough to hold two seahs of seed" (1 Kings 18:32, NKJV). One seah was equivalent to about 31 cups.

He placed the wood and then took the bull sacrifice that had been cut up and laid it on top of the wood. Then he did something interesting. He told them to douse the whole sacrifice and the area around the altar with water. He said, "'Fill four waterpots with water, and pour it on the burnt sacrifice and on the wood.' Then he said, 'Do it a second time,' and they did it a second time; and he said, 'Do it a third time,' and they did it a third time. So the water ran all around the altar; and he also filled the trench with water" (1 Kings 18:33-35, NKJV). Again, we see the three times.

This occurred in the middle of a drought. Imagine the people standing around with their dry mouths and parched throats and staring at all that precious water poured out not once but three times. Elijah wanted to make sure the whole area was saturated so there would be no doubt from where the fire came. He was setting the stage. He wasn't worried about the scarcity of water and what a valuable commodity it was. He knew the drought was ending soon.

Next, Elijah did what he did best; he prayed a simple earnest prayer. When it comes to prayer, the posture of the heart is always most important, not a performance. He says, "'Lord God of Abraham, Isaac, and Israel, let it be known this day that You are God in Israel and I am Your servant, and that I have done all these things at Your word. Hear me, O Lord, hear me, that this people may know that You are the Lord God, and that You have turned their hearts back to You again'" (1 Kings 18:36-37, NKJV).

What happened next was the mountaintop miracle. "Then the fire of the Lord fell and consumed the burnt sacrifice, and the wood and the stones and the dust, and it licked up the water that was in the trench" (1 Kings 18:38, NKJV). The fire acted like it was a living thing. There was no natural explanation for it.

A young shepherd boy slayed a giant with a single stone. A prince of Egypt, turned fugitive murderer, turned humble shepherd, turned hesitant leader, raised a simple wooden staff and parted over 50,000 cubic miles of Red Sea water. So God, at the sixty-three-word prayer of an ordinary man, brought down fire from heaven, and it devoured the water that should have extinguished it. God's fire was so powerful it consumed wood, stones, dust, and flesh along with the water.

What a sight it must have been to witness! There are so many scenes that I want played back for me one day when I get to heaven, and this one is near the top of my list.

"Now when all the people saw it, they fell on their faces; and they said, 'The Lord, He is God! The Lord, He is God!'" (I Kings 18:39, NKJV). Our Father in heaven, is seated on His throne, surrounded by tens of thousands of angelic hosts worshiping Him and praising Him twenty-four/seven, but His gaze is down on us, His wayward creation, for a single shout of sincere and honest praise. He never gives up on us.

Elijah prayed for the miracle to be done so that the people would see God for who He was. How many times do we ask God to do something for us so that it can glorify us and not Him? Let it be for His glory.

Elijah still had a mess to clean up. "And Elijah said to them, 'Seize the prophets of Baal! Do not let one of them escape!' So they seized them; and Elijah brought them down to the Brook Kishon and executed them there" (1 Kings 18:40, NKJV). This mass killing of Baal's prophets may sound harsh. We forget that sin, especially idolatry, is detestable to a Holy God. He is not just the Lamb but also the Lion of Judah. One day a judgment will come upon the earth. It's not here yet because of God's grace and mercy. The influence of Baal's prophets over God's people had to be extinguished publicly and with finality.

There was, however, something else left to accomplish. It was time for it to rain, for the drought and famine to end. "Then Elijah said to Ahab, 'Go up, eat and drink; for there is the sound of the abundance of rain.' So Ahab went up to eat and drink. And Elijah went up to the top of Carmel; then he bowed down to the ground, and put his face between his knees, and said to his servant, 'Go up now, look toward the sea.' So he went up and looked, and said, 'There is nothing.' And seven times he (Elijah) said, 'Go again.' Then it came to pass the seventh time, that he (the servant) said, 'There is a cloud, as small as a man's hand, rising out of the sea!' So he (Elijah) said, 'Go up, say to Ahab, 'Prepare your chariot, and go down before the rain stops you'" (1 Kings 18:41-44, NKJV).

Notice the way Elijah spoke about the rain. He heard it before anyone saw a single cloud in the sky. That's expectancy. He spoke this assurance out loud, and then prayed for the rain. I hope to pray more prayers with this faith. I hope to remember what God says in Isaiah 65:24 (NKJV), "It shall come to pass that before they call, I will answer; And while they are still speaking, I will hear." Before my hands clasp and my knees bend, at the forefront of my mind I want what Jesus says to His disciples in Mark 11:24 (NKJV), "Therefore I say to you, whatever things you ask when you pray, believe that you receive them, and you will have them."

It took one prayer for the fire to come down but seven for the rain. We don't know why. What we do know is that we are commanded to keep praying. First Thessalonians 5:16-18 (NKJV) says, "Rejoice always, pray without ceasing, in everything give thanks; for this is the will of God in Christ Jesus for you." Billy Graham was asked in an interview what he would do differently if he were given the opportunity to live his life over again. He answered wisely, "If I had to do it over again, I'd spend more time in meditation and prayer and just telling the Lord how much I love Him and adore Him…"[3] I imagine Billy Graham prayed a whole lot, and yet he would have prayed more.

Notice how Ahab was left alive, and not only that, but Elijah also advised him when to eat and drink and when to get up and get moving so that he wouldn't get stuck in the rain. In Exodus 33:18 (NKJV), God said to Moses, "… I will be gracious to whom I will be gracious, and I will have compassion on whom I will have compassion." I think Ahab was shown a whole lot of grace here. Only God can see through to the heart of a man, and I wonder what God saw that made Him hold back His wrath from this wicked king. I wonder if Ahab was grateful at all. He'd lost and then witnessed the slaughter of his entire posse, but he was spared. God can take us out at any time. If you're still alive tomorrow morning, you've been given time and another chance that you haven't necessarily earned.

When I was in my early twenties, I was in a car accident on I-45 where my car was totaled. I had been driving 60-70mph, and my only injuries were bruised shins and later, some whiplash. It all transpired quickly, within seconds. I remember my car ended up facing traffic but safely tucked to the side, on the shoulder. No other cars or people had been involved. A construction worker came running down the freeway from where he'd been working. He opened my banged-up driver's side door, and said, "Child, you've just been blessed!" I couldn't see any blessing with my wrecked car, which I'd had for less than a year, but do you see what he meant? I did later, with hindsight. I wish I could go back in time and say, "Ahab, you've just been blessed."

The rains came, and not just a drizzle. During the time it took the servant to go up to Ahab and give him Elijah's directions, "… the sky became black with clouds and wind, and there was heavy rain" (1 Kings

18:45, NKJV). At the earnest, unrelenting prayer of an ordinary man, the drought and famine were over.

Ahab rode away to Jezreel, and something unusual happened to Elijah. "Then the hand of the Lord came upon Elijah; and he girded up his loins and ran ahead of Ahab to the entrance of Jezreel" (1 Kings 18:46, NKJV). God granted Elijah supernatural cardio power that allowed him to run faster than Ahab's horses. To gird up one's loins means to prepare oneself for a task, maybe also to tuck up a long robe so it doesn't get in the way. It was leg day, and Elijah had to engage his core and sprint like a bat out of you know where. God wanted Elijah to get to Jezreel before Ahab did because He knew Ahab was going to tell Jezebel everything that went down on Mount Carmel.

Chapter Four

OUR FRIEND, ELIJAH, AN INSECURE MAN

Of course, when Jezebel heard all about the execution of her prophets, she was furious. Her message to Elijah was clear, "'So let the gods do to me, and more also, if I do not make your life as the life of one of them by tomorrow about this time'" (1 Kings 19:2, NKJV). She was out for his blood.

Elijah took off like the hounds of hell were on his heels, which meant more cardio for him but no mention of the hand of the Lord helping him this time. "...He arose and ran for his life, and went to Beersheba, which belongs to Judah, and left his servant there. But he himself went a day's journey into the wilderness and came and sat down under a broom tree. And he prayed that he might die" (1 Kings 19:4, NKJV).

He sat down under a broom tree and asked to die. Our friend, anointed as he was, because he was an ordinary person like us, lost all his confidence. Our boy E was like, *put a fork in me, God, I'm done.*

"I have had enough, Lord," Elijah said.

Have you ever found yourself saying the same? I know I have.

I wonder what it was that drove my BC brother-in-Christ Elijah to despair on his knees beneath that broom tree. Ahab and Jezebel had hunted him before. He was used to hiding and being on the run. What was different this time?

He struck me as being strong and confident on that mountaintop. What happened to extinguish the fight in him? Was he exhausted and just weary of it being one thing after another?

I think the feeling of isolation got to him. There was no one with him to share the weight of his calling. There was no shoulder to lean on. No one was available to text or call. We know at some point he acquired a servant, but that company wasn't enough to quench his loneliness, since loneliness does not depend on how many people are around you. You can feel alone in a room full of people. You can be lonely in a marriage. You can be a teenager in a big family and still feel completely alone, like no one gets you. Elijah believed he was the only prophet of God, but this was an untrue belief.

Remember Obadiah's conversation with Elijah? Obadiah revealed to Elijah that he'd protected a hundred of God's prophets. Elijah didn't respond to that statement or offer any acknowledgement. There were other prophets of Jehovah. He wasn't the only one. What should have been a relief to him didn't register.

Elijah had also ordered the death of hundreds of men, the prophets of Baal and Asherah. The Lord did not want him to leave them alive because they had turned His people away from Him and would likely try to do it again. It was a terrible deed that had to be done. I wonder if the blood shed at Elijah's verbal order weighed on him too.

1 Kings 19:4 (NKJV) says that Elijah "prayed that he might die." He was asking God to end his life, to put a stop to his misery. In verse 5, he says, "Now, Lord, take my life..."

Can we be so bold with God, so raw, so unpolished, so un-churchlike?

Of course we can. Pastor Steven Furtick once said, "God can't bless who you pretend to be."[4] Give him your mess and see how He responds. Leave that up to Him.

Don't think you are a better Christian because you think poorly of yourself. Insecurity and humility are not the same. In fact, I've heard that pride and insecurity are flip sides of the same coin – preoccupation with self.

And Rick Warren wrote, "True humility is not thinking less of yourself, it's thinking of yourself less."[5]

Do not think that you are a bad Christian because you have experienced anxiety or depression? Read the Psalms and see how much David suffered. The prophet Jeremiah is believed to have written the book of Lamentations. Pastors also battle low self-esteem, depression, feelings of inadequacy, and lack of fulfillment. With that in mind, you should encourage your pastor more often and complain less. Even Charles Spurgeon admitted to having depression. He's quoted in Diana Gruver's article as follows:

> It is a great gift to have learned by experience how to sympathize. "Ah!" I say to them, "I have been where you are!" They look at me and their eyes say, "No, surely you never felt as we do." I therefore go further, and say, "If you feel worse than I did, I pity you, indeed, for I could say with Job, 'My soul chooses strangling rather than life.' I could readily enough have laid violent hands upon myself to escape my misery of spirit.[6]

Jesus says, "Come to Me, all you who labor and are heavy laden, and I will give you rest. Take My yoke upon you and learn from Me, for I am gentle and lowly in heart, and you will find rest for your souls" (Matthew 11:28-29, NKJV).

God's response to this weary man who took himself too seriously was one of kindness and compassion. He knew Elijah's frailty, just like He knows ours. God wanted the pain offered up to Him. He wanted to be included in that part. It's a relationship, you see.

"Then as he lay and slept under a broom tree, suddenly an angel touched him, and said to him, 'Arise and eat.' Then he looked, and there by his head was a cake baked on coals, and a jar of water. So he ate and drank, and lay down again. And the angel of the Lord came back the second time, and touched him, and said, 'Arise and eat, because the journey is too great for you.' So he arose, and ate and drank; and he went in the strength of that food forty days and forty nights as far as Horeb, the mountain of God" (1 Kings 19:5-10, NKJV).

It sounds like Elijah just needed a snack and a nap, but it's something deeper than that. He was suicidal. This larger-than-life Biblical hero was depressed and anxious to the point that he wanted to die. He was an ordinary man at the end of his own strength, at the end of himself, and that is when God took over as a compassionate father. He met Elijah's physical needs, too. The one meal and sleep were not enough to replenish him; he must have been exhausted. A common symptom of depression is tiredness. Elijah had performed a miracle, executed criminals, and completed a high-intensity cardio workout. He was coming down from quite the adrenaline rush.

Author Hannah Brencher posted, "In Luke Chapter 8, Jesus raises a girl from the dead. I've read this story about 1,000 times but there's a line I hadn't noticed before: 'He took her by the hand and said, 'My child, get up!' Her spirit returned, and at once she stood up. Then Jesus told them to give her something to eat.' Jesus told them to give her something to eat? Why is that line in there, I wondered. Jesus just performed the ultimate miracle and he wants them to get her some food? I feel like God nudged me in that moment to see something I'd never noticed before: physical health is deeply intertwined with spiritual and mental health. So often we get stuck in the spiritual but Jesus is saying, right here, that our physical health must also be examined. It is part of the healing process." [7]

Elijah's soul was weary, and his body was weak. God recognized both. He took care of the physical need; He didn't neglect it. Elijah was afraid and probably tired of feeling that fear. God met him at the point of his weakness. He didn't wait for him to clean himself up. Elijah was His child, and He cared for him, protected him and met his immediate needs. God loves us the same way. He is the God who can send fire down from heaven, and He is the God who comforts us.

"Blessed be the God and Father of our Lord Jesus Christ, the Father of mercies and God of all comfort..." (2 Corinthians 1:3, NKJV).

Elijah was strengthened there in the same place he was prepared to bid farewell to the wretchedness he thought was his life. He believed he was at the end, but God knew him better than he knew himself. This was not how or where he was meant to go. God wasn't done with him yet. He had planned a more glorious return home to heaven for His beloved prophet.

Elijah traveled on from under that desert shrub to Mount Horeb. We will discuss later the intimate conversation between God and this ordinary man that occurred in that sacred place. That is where God addressed Elijah's spiritual need.

Like Elijah, I've found myself under my own broom tree. Every time, God would give me a gentle push to grab a pen and paper and write down what He shared with my heart there. Second Corinthians 1:3 (NKJV) in its entirety says, "Blessed be the God and Father of our Lord Jesus Christ, the Father of mercies and God of all comfort, who comforts us in all our tribulation, **that we may be able to comfort those who are in any trouble, with the comfort with which we ourselves are comforted by God**." (emphasis added). As God gave me the courage to share the lessons and the comfort I learned in those seasons under the broom tree, the vision of this book took shape in my mind. Jesus helped me overcome my doubts and fears about writing something so personal. He revealed it to me as an opportunity to share my testimony.

Here are the circumstances, the events, which brought me under the broom tree. Perhaps you have found yourself in similar situations.

Chapter Five

WHOSE AM I?

When I forget whose I am...

There are times I've forgotten my identity, my true self, until I'm finally brought to my knees, defeated and exhausted.

As soon as we enter this world, we are known as someone's daughter, someone's sister, but when you were created, God called you His. You are His forevermore; you are a child of God and so am I. You were born with a void in your heart that is cut out in the shape of God's love. Until you learn to fill it with this, you will attempt to fill it with all manner of replacements that fall short. It's like a toy that toddlers play with, an empty box with openings cut into different shapes such as hearts, squares, and triangles. The child is supposed to put each block into its proper-shaped opening. When you try to insert something other than God into His space in your heart, you are like that toddler struggling to put a square-shaped piece into the heart-shaped opening, and you, much like that small child, will become frustrated.

I'll never forget the day that started me on a soul search to figure this out. A little background story first. I was born and raised in Texas, and if y'all know anyone who is Texas-bred like yours truly, you know that we live and die in Texas. I was transplanted to Florida in my late twenties via marriage to my then husband who was a Florida native, or "Flo-grown" as many a bumper sticker here displayed. Because we shared two beautiful boys whose primary residence was Florida, returning to the Republic of Texas wasn't in the cards for me, no matter how desperately my heart yearned for it. I was a stranger to this place. I often referred to Florida as "the swamp," since snakes and alligators were part of the everyday landscape. The natives weren't freaked out about them, which was completely unnatural to me. Everyone I called friend in Florida identified me through my former partner. I was so-and-so's wife, and then after our divorce, his ex-wife.

Divorce in the Indian community, though it's unfortunately becoming more common, holds a greater stigma than in the Western or American culture. It's very hard for people to stay completely neutral in a divorce. Most people will favor one of the partners. The preference is sometimes based on the reason for the divorce itself and who is at greater fault. Sometimes it's the length of history and time spent with one person versus the other; it's usually one of these aspects that creates the bias. It's only natural that mutual friends favor one spouse over the other. Who do you invite to your anniversary party or your kid's birthday party, the ex-husband or the ex-wife?

Fortunately for my ex-husband and me, once the unpleasant dust had settled, we would let the other person know when there was an event that the boys might enjoy. Whichever of us had them that weekend or at that time would usually take them. Besides, it wasn't like we couldn't stand being in the same room with each other. We could both be at a school function together, even save a seat for the other person, and I think our boys did much better because of our amicability.

After the divorce, I hoped for people to get to know me as an individual, for my identity to be a new thing not tied to another person. After a while, I was sure I was achieving this, but one conversation derailed this certainty.

I'll never forget the warm, sunny Florida afternoon about a year after the divorce when I was at a mutual friend's familiar, comfortable home for a get-together. There were mostly Indian people gathered, talking and laughing over plates of rice and delicious curries. Indian communities tend to be close-knit. Most of the people there were ones I'd known for several years, or at least had been acquainted with, but there were a few new, unfamiliar faces for me.

I'd noticed one of those unknowns, a woman in her late sixties, was watching me with a curious expression.

After I'd smiled and nodded a hello at her, she approached me. "Aunty" was what I called her, because in Indian culture, almost every woman who was possibly old enough to be your mother but wasn't your mother was referred to as "Aunty". She'd never met me before, and the first words out of her mouth floored me. A simple three-word question managed to fluster me and fill my mind with uncertainty.

"Whose are you?"

I'd never been asked such a thing by anyone before. My mouth may have hung open slightly for a few awkward seconds. Maybe she just wanted to know my name, I thought, so I gave her my name, but she shook her head and asked more emphatically, "Okay, but *whose* are you?"

Feeling uncomfortable, with red cheeks and a nervous smile, my confidence began to sink as I attempted to explain that I was such-and-such person's friend. She smiled back tolerantly and persisted, "Yes, we are all friends here, but *whose* are you?" I didn't want to answer that I was so-and-so's ex-wife, not after more than a year of establishing myself as my own person, but that is what I ended up declaring: I was so-and-so's ex-wife. And that's what it took for her to finally identify me. That marriage association was what satisfied her question.

Was that truly whose I was? Where did I fit in now? Was that all there was to me, that I'd been married and was now a divorced, single mom?

The question at that party struck me on such a deeper level. Whose was I now? I had been a daughter, a sister, a doctor, a mother, a wife, and then an ex-wife. Did I keep identifying myself by the people who were in my life or by my occupation, or did I have an identity that was greater than that?

Merriam-Webster's definition of identity is, "the distinguishing character or personality of an individual." It's a word that's been thrown around and discussed on many platforms. If I identify myself as a doctor, what happens to that identity if a lawsuit causes me to lose my medical license? Or if I'm injured and can't practice as a doctor, then what am I? I still go on. I still live, but if I've placed my identity on something that is breakable, on a foundation that is neither firm nor eternal, then who am I? I am a woman, a genetic female, sure, but is that all I am?

We are created and purposefully designed to identify as children of God. Any other foundational identifier will make us insecure at our core. It will leave us treading water in a bottomless ocean. Our feet will struggle to find some solid ground. We will come to the end of ourselves under the broom tree with Elijah. He thought himself the one and only prophet of God, the only believer left, all false beliefs. God met him when he was on his knees and showed him that he was much more than that. Elijah was loved as God's child, as His intentional creation, and that identity was not only enough, it was everything.

You can't allow an event in your life to become your identity.

When people in my culture called me a "woman of divorce", I felt the condemnation in those words. I felt the burden of them, the chains they set on me. Yet it wasn't them, it was Satan -- the enemy -- using them to condemn me and make me forget who I am. I am who my Father in heaven says I am, and so are you.

If you believe lies long and hard enough, they'll lead you to a dark pit. And that is where the enemy wants you. He hopes you will listen to what he has to say when you're down in that space.

I'm a pediatrician with almost twenty years of experience in the field, and I noticed a trend emerging in a certain population of my patients. I started seeing more boys, and especially girls, in their 'tweens and teen years with anxiety and depression. Their symptoms, though they made sense to me as a physician, began to burden my heart as a Christian. These kids could not see themselves as their Heavenly Father saw them. They were trying to measure up by the world's standards and loathed themselves for falling short. I knew in my spirit that it was part of the enemy's plot for their lives that they would be constantly distracted. With their confidence kept down, they'd never realize their true worth in this world, never see themselves as their Father sees them, never fulfill His purpose for them. Some of them seemed so lost and defeated. I saw myself in them when I was their age.

Be careful whom you find, who seems to pop into your life, when your expectations are diminished, when your thoughts of yourself are low. Have caution of whom you let into your circle and into your weary heart. Be wary of the words, the information you are fed, and the thoughts that those words create in your mind.

Young people nowadays have too much information but not enough truth at their fingertips, and their earnest search for truth, sifting through the onslaught of words and images, leaves them misguided and often confused. Children and adolescents are mercurial. They're developing and learning and wiring their brains. There's a lot of change that happens between when they're nervously attending their first day of preschool to when they are walking across a stage to accept their high school diploma.

Feelings change, and no matter how strong they are, they are not truth. A certain song can put you in a sullen mood, but another song can lift your spirits, and another one can make you feel like dancing.

I've seen so many young people who sensed that they didn't feel right in their body, like what they saw somehow contradicted what they felt. In a way that's nothing new. Everyone has to figure out who they are. Except what happens in this day and age of abundant false information when a young person searches for their identity? What's trending? The suggestion that maybe they're the wrong gender. The idea that they were somehow created wrong and that God just made a mistake. Or maybe they will learn that they'll never be acknowledged or loved because they don't meet a certain cultural standard of beauty, or because they don't have the same talents as a wealthy person they follow.

When I started practicing in pediatrics twenty years ago, I came across maybe one or two transgender patients. That number quadrupled for me in the past five years, yet I always affirmed whatever gender the patient said he or she was and used whatever pronouns that person used. I followed the rules set out by the top organizations in medicine. Then something happened to make me question what I was doing.

I had a patient change her mind. She was assigned female gender at birth and decided she was transgender in her teens. I followed the guidelines and affirmed the male gender, sent her to psychiatry and endocrinology, and both confirmed the diagnosis. Her family was supportive. She started testosterone. Then a few years later she changed her mind. She didn't change her mind due to social pressure. She had a supportive family. When she was questioning her identity, she was influenced by what she saw on the internet and on social media. Later as a young adult who understood herself better, she decided that she was a bisexual female.

That's not supposed to happen, right? But it did. I witnessed it and was at a loss for how to proceed with other patients who were coming to me as transgender.

Why are so many kids coming out as transgender now than there were a decade ago? I think a lot of the kids who are saying they are transgender are more "questioning" than truly transgender. I think they search for what they are on social media and prematurely come to the conclusion that they are transgender when they really aren't. I think they have doubts about their identity, and they are questioning.

Social media has had a tremendous influence on how kids see themselves and the world around them. I don't think we realize just how immense and unquantifiable the impact of social media is on young people. Look at what the Tik Tok challenges can make people do, not just kids but adults as well. Some of these are all in fun, but others have proven dangerous.

I was never transgender, but I did believe that my body was wrong, that I was made the wrong way, a mistake, and a blunder on God's part. I believed that no one could love me the way I was. It was impossible. There were many words said at me, over me, and about women in general that stuck with me, and when I looked back, the origins of my self-hatred, like a twisted, thorny, thick vine, grew from those words. They encircled me and held me trapped and bleeding. I'll mention a few to give you an idea.

When I was a tween, two aunties who were at a get-together at my parents' house were discussing my sister and me and whom they liked better. They spoke in Malayalam and assumed that because I was born in the United States I wouldn't understand the language. Little did they know, my first language was not English, it was Malayalam, and even though I spoke it with an American accent at the time, I understood it well. They said they liked my sister better because she was lighter-skinned. I was the dark one, and it wounded me as a kid to think that someone liked me less because my skin was darker. They weren't the only ones in my life to comment negatively on my skin tone.

When I was a young teen, I was a late bloomer. I was boxy-shaped with broad shoulders, a chubby belly, and narrow hips. I knew I looked different from other girls my age who were shapelier. I was insecure, so I would carefully cut out the shoulder pads of my tops and dresses because I definitely didn't need them. If you recall, shoulder pads were all the rage in the 80s. I wore a brown suede jacket through every season of tenth grade in humid Houston, Texas to hide my body shape. Then an adult who was close to me, someone I trusted, said that I wasn't shaped how a woman should be shaped. What a messed up thing to say to a kid! Those words stuck with me and solidified this belief in my mind that my body was wrong.

A boy who sat at a desk across from me in Spanish class called me a "big fat beach ball". The class heard, and there was quiet laughter. The teacher did nothing. I wanted to disappear altogether. It wasn't the first or last fat comment thrown at me, just another one of many reinforcing ones. A few years later, another teenage boy made the offhand comment that I didn't walk like a girl should walk. And another commented, "You don't dress or act like how a girl should."

Thank goodness I was a teen in the late 80s and early 90s and not in the 2020s so I had no Google or Instagram to reference. I believed I was malformed. With all the faulty thinking going around in my mind, what would I have found if I had searched for why my body was wrong?

If you come out as transgender on social media, you may get thousands of likes from strangers who suddenly support you. There are kids who create videos of themselves taking "T" or testosterone, and they get so many views and likes, and they are trending. It feels good to most people to be seen, acknowledged, validated, liked.

Transgender isn't the same as being gay or lesbian. It has nothing to do with to whom you are attracted or whom you love. Yet the "T" is added to the end of LGBQ-T. The rare true transgender more likely has a biological origin, but that's not what we are seeing coming into our offices in record numbers. I do believe that true transgender exists. There are people who may be born the wrong gender just like there are people with mixed gonadal dysgenesis (MGD) and complete androgen insensitivity syndrome (CAIS), both of which are genetic disorders that affect growth and development before and after birth, but I also know these are all extremely rare.

Merriam-Webster defines *gay* as "of, relating to, or characterized by sexual or romantic attraction to people of one's same sex," and *lesbian* as "of, relating to, or characterized by sexual or romantic attraction to other women or between women."

The same dictionary defines *transgender* as "of, relating to, or being a person whose gender identity differs from the sex the person had or was identified as having at birth." Being transgender has nothing to do with to whom you are attracted, but they are grouped with gays and lesbians. I don't know a gay man who wants his penis removed or a lesbian woman who hates her own vagina.

I found more stories of how some patients regretted taking hormones and undergoing surgery, and I wondered if these people were actually questioning, and not truly transgender, which, again, exists but is very rare.

Transgenders should be protected from discrimination and so should the people who are questioning. Their pain is real and it's debilitating. It is truly distressing for these kids to feel like they are the wrong gender or that their body is wrong. There is a pressure on them when they are forced to conform to the gender they were assigned at birth when they believe it is wrong. I want them to have hope. I don't want any more kids to take their own lives over this. After what I've seen, I wonder about the true source of the increased numbers of transgender and questioning kids.

Every belief we have originates with a thought. The thought that they are the wrong gender becomes a solid belief and not many people are asking why. I think we are missing the mark and doing them a disservice.

Why did they start to believe they were the wrong gender? I think these kids need to be free to question. There should be more available, specially-trained therapists who are willing to dig deep, specialists who talk to them early on about why they question, not ones who are letting the hour pass to collect a copay or ones telling them they are whatever they feel they are. Let the kids cut their hair how they want and wear gender-neutral clothes if they want, but go slowly on the treatments that have irreversible effects.

Sex hormones like testosterone and estrogen are effective. They create change quickly, and this appeals to the mercurial nature of children and adolescents. There's a novelty euphoria that comes with taking these hormones. One makes hair sprout up out of nowhere and deepens your voice, the other makes your breasts grow. Neither is without consequences.

We know that children and adolescents are not good at considering the long-term consequences of their short-term decisions. Don't sniff that; it may cause brain damage. Don't smoke that; it can cause lung damage later. So when we counsel distressed kids about hormones and say taking them may cause infertility later, they may insist they are fine with that future consequence, but do they really get it? How do you know they really understand how they'll feel about infertility in twenty years when they are in a loving relationship with a partner and when they see their friends start families?

There are parents who are quick to start their kids on these hormones but refuse the HPV vaccine which protects against cancer because they "heard" it could cause infertility (which isn't true, by the way). What happens to an eleven-year-old boy who starts estrogen? His testicles won't develop, his penis won't grow, and he will develop breast tissue and an increased risk of breast cancer. What happens if he changes his mind when he's twenty and decides he's a male? Now he can't have children naturally, has extra breast tissue that will have to be removed surgically, and has a penis and testicles the size of a child's.

When a child or adolescent thinks he or she was born the wrong gender, before that develops into a strong belief, should we focus only on changing his or her outward appearance, or should we be digging deeper and working harder to find a way for them to address why they believe this way? We shouldn't prioritize their psychological reality or how they feel. If a six-foot tall, two-hundred-pound Caucasian boy identifies as a petite Asian female, we shouldn't do whatever possible to make his psychological reality (petite Asian female) match his physical reality (tall, two hundred pound Caucasian male) just because we can.

Are we asking the right questions? Is there more going on behind-the-scenes that we aren't digging into? Is anyone finding out if they were sexually abused or if someone said an offhand comment about their appearance that they fixated on? Is there a strained relationship with a parent, a parent who is not emotionally involved at all, or one who is physically distant?

The following is not a transgender story, but it is a good example of why it's important to find out what is going on in someone's life that leads to a certain way of thinking, believing and behaving. I had a mom bring her young son in for aggression, especially towards her. He had social impairment with other kids. She wondered if he had autism. Several months later, the mom let me know that she had left her husband because of domestic violence. So this boy was witnessing his dad beating up his mom. Of course he was aggressive towards his mom. He was imitating what he was seeing. He was demonstrating his pain in the only way he knew how, but we didn't catch it until his mom bravely admitted what was happening in the home. He couldn't get better until she took him out of that situation. We could have put him on different medications to regulate his emotions, but until we addressed the source of his distress, he wasn't going to have the best outcome.

To distinguish the true, rare transgender, we need to go slower and not be in a hurry to start hormones which may have some potentially irreversible consequences. Support these kids and give them better guidance. When did the questioning start and why? Is there trauma? Let them feel safe to talk openly about anything that they've seen or experienced., and this takes time to sort out. We need to speak truth into their lives while they question, before it clicks over to a solid belief.

The data show that once these kids develop the solid belief that they are the wrong gender, then affirming the gender they believe they are will be what helps them the most to stay alive. There's growing evidence that it saves their lives, and according to the 2015 US Transgender Survey, only 5% of those who had transitioned to another gender decided to de-transition and go back to the gender they were assigned at birth. I think that is because something clicks over in their minds, and then it's lifesaving to affirm the gender they believe they are.

I don't believe in conversion therapy, which sounds horrifying. I don't advocate that. I believe in diving into quality therapy when they start to question, but that can be difficult to find for most people.

If your self-worth is attached to your weight, you can develop an eating disorder. I've sat across from an anorexic while she pinched the loose skin on her emaciated arm and said, "If I could just get rid of this fat, if I could just remove it, then I would be happy." Would it be right for me to oblige her? We know it won't make her better, and just giving her extra calories won't make her better either. Sure the calories to get her up to a healthy weight would normalize her ECG and correct her electrolyte panel, but they won't fix the real underlying issue.

The issue is this solid belief that she is fat no matter what the scale says or what the mirror shows. The belief is like a voice, and once it is there, it's never silenced. The way to help her is to develop a louder voice that reminds her the first voice is wrong. That takes years of therapy and support, and it's a lifelong struggle. An anorexic's pain is just as real as that of the kid who thinks they are in the wrong body. What if we are dealing with similar issues?

I've seen a pattern emerge. When we over-focus on one aspect of ourselves, whether it's our weight, gender, etc., we distort it. And when we attach that aspect to something emotional like our self-worth, we lose our identity.

What lies and misinformation would we be free of if we understood, not just in our minds, but deep down inside our hearts, in the marrow of our bones, who we are to God? Instead of identifying ourselves based on gender or race or life-event, if we first and foremost oriented ourselves as a child of God, what would we be free of?

Our culture has tried to over-sexualize children and pressure them to grow up way too fast. Young children don't need to be quizzed repeatedly on what gender they feel they are and who they are sexually attracted to so they can acquire a highly specific, multi-hyphenated label. What kind of perverted grooming is that? We have focused so much on how we relate to each other sexually that we have forgotten how to relate to each other as human beings.

Mark Batterson in his book, *Whisper: How to Hear the Voice of God*, said, "All our identity issues are fundamental misunderstandings of who God is. Guilt issues are a misunderstanding of God's grace. Control issues are a misunderstanding of God's sovereignty. Anger issues are a misunderstanding of Gods mercy. Pride issues are a misunderstanding of God's greatness. Trust issues are a misunderstanding of God's goodness. If you struggle with any of those issues, it's time to let God be the loudest voice in your life!"[8]

My identity doesn't exist in being a cisgender heterosexual female. I'm a child of God, first and foremost. Believing that in my spirit and in my soul has released me from so much pain and doubt. I don't believe I'm in the wrong body anymore. Even if I don't conform to the current cultural ideal of beauty, the One who has the final say in how I look is the same One who created me thoughtfully and intentionally. He says those aspects of me don't mean much when it comes to my identity. They aren't greater just because I over-focus on them. When I look in the mirror, there may be a voice that still tells me my shoulders are too broad for a girl and that my skin is too dark, but there's the more powerful voice of the Holy Spirit of Almighty God that assures me that the breadth of my shoulders and the color of my skin matter very little when it comes to whose I am.

Chapter Six

THE THRONE OF MY HEART

When I've put something else on the throne instead of God...

Losing focus of what was most important, my relationship with God, has led me to my knees many a time.

I grew up in a Christian home. There were pictures of Jesus on the walls, crosses set up in various places, and the traditional Last Supper picture in the dining room. I even attended church sometimes. My parents did not take us every week, yet somehow I always managed to show up to Sunday school during memory verse competition day or singing competition day or one of the written exam days. If it was memory verse competition day, I would use the regulars like, "The Lord is my shepherd and I shall not want," and "Jesus wept," (the shortest verse in the Bible FYI) and I would recite the *Lord's Prayer*, which to my teachers for some reason only counted as one verse. Go figure. The worst was the singing competition because I couldn't carry a tune to save my life and always messed up lyrics to songs. I still do.

So I grew up knowing Jesus in my mind, but I'd never encountered Him in my heart. While attending college at the University of Texas at Austin, a friend invited me to a Bible study, and I started going weekly. The youth pastor who led the meetings was young, energetic and engaging. He talked about Jesus in a down-to-earth way that I'd never heard before. Jesus became real to me in those hours. So in that dusty, fluorescent-lit meeting room at one of the campus dormitories, I made my decision. I was broken enough and open enough to fully understand my need for His saving grace. At the age of twenty, after attending church my entire life, I finally spoke aloud that I accepted Jesus as my Savior.

But old habits don't immediately die once you accept Him.

Even after I accepted Jesus as my Savior, it took years to understand the concept of the throne. The word "throne" in Greek is *thronos* and means "elevated seat." The New Oxford American Dictionary defines it as "a ceremonial chair for a sovereign, bishop or similar figure." What takes the "elevated seat" in our lives? What is set apart and placed as sovereign? Is it money, another person, or a pursuit? Are we consumed with our feelings and ourselves? Are we confusing our feelings for truth?

One way to see who sits on the throne of your heart is to ask yourself, "Who defines my worth?" If how you feel about yourself is determined by how well your favorite pair of jeans fit or the number on a scale, then you, or more specifically your appearance, is on the throne. If your self-worth depends on how many things you finished on your to-do list, then your accomplishments are on the throne, or better yet, being in control. If your self-worth depends on having a man in your life and what his opinion is of you, then that man is on the throne. There is nothing wrong with being a healthy weight and being conscientious about grooming and appearance, but they have a subordinate place in our lives and should not be our greatest priority. They should not have the authority in how we go about our day and how we interact with others. There is nothing wrong with being successful and efficient in daily tasks, but your value as a person doesn't hang there. God is still God regardless of how you look or what you are able to get done.

I wasn't ready to dethrone myself and make Jesus the absolute authority over my life. There were things in the Bible that I wanted to believe were outdated and irrelevant for current times. I disobeyed, sought out the temporary fixes for loneliness, and pursued whatever desire seemed greatest at the time. These ultimately left me feeling empty and lonelier.

When you give up your own authority and make Jesus the King over your life, you start wanting to obey Him because you love Him. When you want to obey Him out of love, you seek out what He wants for you and what His opinion of you is. The only place you can find that is in His word. You will naturally seek His word once He has the authority and your full attention.

"I praise You because I am fearfully and wonderfully made; Your works are wonderful, I know that full well" (Psalm 139:14, NIV).

I would encourage every woman to write that verse on a post-it note and stick it on her mirror. We should speak those words over ourselves daily. I had read that verse many times growing up, but I didn't experience the truth of it until it was spoken to me personally by a mentor and dear friend of mine. It can still be a rough, arduous process tuning out the negatives when I get dressed in the morning.

A statistic I read recently said that the average American woman is 5 feet 4 inches tall and weighs around 140 pounds, and the average clothing size for a woman in America is between a size 12 and 14. The average woman's waist size is around 37.8 inches. That's the reality of our measurements. What is society's ideal? There is some variation about what is ideal according to different cultures, but let's look at an epitome of beauty: the supermodel. The ideal height is to be 5 feet 9 inches and have a 24-inch waistline. A size 6 model is considered "plus size".

But you are "fearfully and wonderfully made" in God's image. The word "fearfully" here means with great respect and reverence. This means God took time in deciding how much hair you would have on your head and what color it would be. There was reverence for the particulars. You have a heart that beats and a mind that thinks. You have a spirit that can be moved. And they all work a certain way because that's how He wanted you to be. He included the minutia with great respect.

Ephesians 1:4-5 (NIV) says, "For He chose us in Him before the creation of the world to be holy and blameless in His sight. In love He predestined us to be adopted as his sons (and daughters) through Jesus Christ..." So we are chosen, and as chosen people, we are formed with great respect and reverence. Knowing this should make you realize that you are not here randomly. God wants you to know who you really are to Him. You have great value and purpose, regardless of how you feel about yourself, regardless of how you came into this world, and regardless of what anyone has said about you in the past.

Some of the labels I received growing up were "fat" and "dark". For an Indian woman, the world tells you that dark skin is undesirable. The skin-lightening industry is worth millions of dollars in India because there is a demand for light skin. For an overweight girl who liked to play outside in the sun, this was a hard burden to bear. I was plagued with the choice of whether or not I should play outside and ride my bike in the blazing sunshine of the Deep South. I needed to burn off the extra weight, but then that would have just tanned my brown skin even more. Ultimately, I chose to play outside and continue eating a lot of food, so I was made fun of incessantly for my appearance. I think a lot of women can relate to that. I grew up looking in the mirror seeing an overweight, dark-skinned girl and continued to keep that image of myself for years after.

The negative self-talk didn't stop when the weight came off due to healthier eating and learning to enjoy exercise. My skin naturally lightened due to spending more time indoors studying, but I still saw myself as undesirable and just plain rejected.

Are you measuring worth by the amount of beauty you perceive in yourself? Are you adding greater worth to other people than the worth you see in yourself because you perceive them as having greater physical beauty? As a woman, do you sometimes think, "He would never look at me. I'm not pretty enough for him." I know I have many times.

I'm also guilty of the reverse. There were times when a friend suggested I talk to a man who was conventionally good-looking, meaning "a tall, dark, and handsome" man. I thought such a man would never be interested in me because I wasn't pretty enough, and I would judge his heart. I'd assume he was superficial and egotistic, probably a womanizer, and that he had never known heartache or rejection in his life. Incredibly presumptuous, I know, but it was my way of disqualifying him.

How does this change? How do we stop beating ourselves up over what we see in our reflection? How do we stop judging others based on their looks? How do we stop comparing ourselves to the ideals of beauty on television, on social media, and in magazines? Let me tell you that it doesn't happen overnight, and the process has to be done intentionally and repetitively. New pathways have to be forged in your thinking.

The answer I found was in speaking God's truth over my insecurities. There is power in the Word of God. It has the ability to transform a life of insecurity to one of healthy self-esteem. I am "fearfully and wonderfully made". I am the daughter of a king. I am created in the image of the holy and mighty God. Any time those old labels raise their unwelcome heads, push them out with His truth, and speak His Word over the situation – and I'll use the words again, *intentionally, repetitively.*

His opinion of you is in His Word, which is the Bible. You have to open it and read it, or you can open the app for it on your handheld device. I would encourage you to read and find the words for yourself, but here are a few:

"For I know the thoughts that I think toward you, says the Lord, thoughts of peace and not of evil, to give you a future and a hope" (Jeremiah 29:11, NKJV).

"Know that the Lord, He is God; It is He who has made us, and not we ourselves; We are His people and the sheep of His pasture" (Psalm 100:3, NKJV).

"When my father and my mother forsake me, then the Lord will take care of me" (Psalm 27:10, NKJV).

"For we are His workmanship, created in Christ Jesus for good works, which God prepared beforehand that we should walk in them" (Ephesians 2:10, NKJV).

"The Lord your God in your midst, the Mighty One, will save; He will rejoice over you with gladness, He will quiet you with His love, He will rejoice over you with singing" (Zephaniah 3:17, NKJV).

"For God has not given us a spirit of fear, but of power and of love and of a sound mind" (2 Timothy 1:7, NKJV).

"But those who wait on the Lord shall renew their strength; They shall mount up with wings like eagles, They shall run and not be weary, They shall walk and not faint" (Isaiah 40:31, NKJV).

"My flesh and my heart fail; But God is the strength of my heart and my portion forever" (Psalm 73:26, NKJV).

When you have found, read, believed, and internalized these words, among the many others in Scripture, the opinions of others from the past, present and future will fade in their importance. You will care more what He thinks. Remember the throne of your heart. When you dethrone yourself and start believing Him, thank God; you dethrone your insecurities about yourself as well. They have no place under His rule. Through the truth of His Word, He teaches you the true beauty that you are as His beloved creation.

I didn't take the path I thought I would in life, but I ended up where I needed to be. I didn't end up in that college Bible study by chance. Jesus led me to a path of building a relationship with Him. I took a journey that transformed me from someone with a religion to someone with a relationship. Being a Christian started becoming more than a box I checked off to best describe my belief system. And I'm far from finished. There's a lot of work to be done. He's leading me still.

God is not hovering at 30,000 feet looking down on you. He is closer than the air you breathe, and He is interested in the minute details of your life. When it comes to you, no detail is trivial to Him. To know Him is to love Him and to realize how unconditionally loved you are. That love is a healing balm for every broken heart. His love for you is always there, overflowing for you, but you have to embrace it.

Chapter Seven

EVERY ROSE HAS ITS THORN

When I struggled with a thorn in my side…

It's more than just a song title from an Eighties rock band. We all have thorns in our sides. I have many, but one that I've felt has beaten me down my entire adult life has been my struggle with alopecia (hair loss).

Indian women are supposed to have thick hair. They're not supposed to have thin hair, and they're definitely not supposed to lose their hair in their late teens. I was diagnosed with autoimmune thyroiditis when I was seventeen years old. One of the symptoms I presented with was hair loss. Through the help of modern medicine and a little tablet called Synthroid, my thyroid disease is controlled. My hair, however, steadily continued to thin.

I hated my hair as a teenager. It was already on the thin side, the strands finely textured and easily frizzed. I wanted better hair so badly. My mom gave me a Catholic prayer booklet when I was about thirteen, and I read about a prayer called a novena. The traditional way for one to pray a novena was to say the same prayer at least once a day for nine consecutive days, and one should try to say it at the same time of day. Back then I thought that Neelam Kothari, a Bollywood actress, had the most beautiful hair. Long, thick, straight and absolutely gorgeous. To me, hers was the epitome of hair for a woman. So I thought, why not pray for the best out there? So my desperate, silly teenage self set an alarm each day for nine days and prayed for hair like Neelam's.

That prayer was not answered. Instead, four years later, I started to lose what hair I had. Talk about disappointment. I hadn't been saved at that time. I'd been to church my whole life but never really knew who God was, and I was disappointed by Him before I even truly got to know Him.

You may think, *big deal, men lose their hair all the time.* And yes they do, but even for an older man, losing his hair is a hit to the self-image. So imagine what it's like for a young woman. I had to set my alarm thirty minutes earlier everyday so that I could arrange my hair in a clip on top of my head to strategically cover the worst areas. There were many days I'd leave with tears in my eyes because it took me longer than the time I had allotted, and I was late to my first class of the day.

I received all kinds of well-intentioned unsolicited advice that I politely smiled through and nodded my head for.

"You should take vitamin E."

"You should take biotin."

I even got recipes for concoctions to massage into my hair. When I was on vacation with my family in India, someone ground up nellikka (Indian gooseberry or amla) and thulassi (holy basil), and she swore to me it would make me grow hair. I was game to try anything back in the day. I've got to say that mixture, when massaged to your scalp on a daily basis, will make your hair grow longer faster. Unfortunately however, it does not grow new hair. I tried topical minoxidil, not just the one for women, but also the one for men because it had a higher potency. It didn't help me. I tried so many hair, skin and nail vitamins. The hair that I had would grow longer faster, but I couldn't grow new hair, and I was consistently, obsessive-compulsively faithful with all these remedies. I was young and full of enthusiasm and energy for something, anything, to help me.

Then there were the rude snickers, funny looks, and the mean comments. Once, when I was in college, I had a particularly uncomfortable experience during a get-together at a friend's house. There I was sitting on the floor just hanging out and minding my business, when a girl sitting on the couch behind me yelled, "Oh my God! She's bald!" Then she pushed my head down so that the people could see some areas on the top of my head that I apparently hadn't covered as well as I'd hoped. I tried to shrug it off and said, "Yeah, my hair is really thin," but I wanted to run out of there. I felt humiliated and exposed.

I went to a national hair loss center in Los Angeles. They did a scalp analysis and confirmed that there was more than just one cause to my thinning hair, which was probably why nothing seemed to really improve it. They said they could help me with a form of hair replacement. I was a medical resident at the time, barely making enough money to pay the bills and monthly rent. When they told me the cost, it was more than I could afford, so I explained that I would like to try it one day, but I just didn't have the means at that time. The tech, or really the sales person who did my consultation, really tried to push me to purchase their plan. He said, "Well, what are you going to do then? Just walk around the way you are? A bald woman is ugly!"

All those hurtful words over the years are burned into my mind to this day. They've left a scar, all because of this thorn that God never took from me, no matter how much I pleaded.

The final whammy to my hair came with the birth of my second son. Not only did my face break out with the worst rosacea and perioral dermatitis of my life, but instead of the thick luxurious hair that most women get while pregnant, my hair started to thin out even more. Some older Indian women believe that if your looks deteriorate during pregnancy, then it means you're going to have a girl because she's "trying to steal your beauty." I can't roll my eyes far enough to the back of my head for that foolishness.

After the birth of my beautiful boy, there was no hiding it. My hair was going. Not just in the areas where there's female pattern baldness, but all over, especially in the front. I couldn't hide it anymore. There was no style in the world to disguise it (not even bangs, which someone suggested).

I felt like people just saw a balding woman. It was the first thing they noticed about me, and the only thing that seemed to matter. Forget that I was a doctor, that I was someone's mom, that I was someone's daughter. There was even a man with male pattern baldness who made fun of me for losing my hair. As if I did this to myself on purpose, as if I didn't spend my entire adult life trying solutions, failing time and time again, and feeling hopeful, only to be crushed over and over.

I didn't need Neelam's hair anymore. I just wanted enough of my own to look like a normal person. I had many one-sided arguments with God about it.

"If You would just let me look normal, I could _____!"

I filled in that blank with what I could do, who I could be, what I could accomplish, but did I need hair to accomplish those things or did I just need God? Do you really need that thing or do you just need God to help you see that thing the way He sees it, with the mind of Christ, not your own mind?

Our thorns keep us humble. Pride in us is the same self-deceiving thinking that made an angel into the devil. It's what made Lucifer fall and become Satan.

"When pride comes, then comes disgrace, but with humility comes wisdom" (Proverbs 11:2, NIV).

"Pride goes before destruction, a haughty spirit before a fall. Better to be lowly in spirit along with the oppressed than to share plunder with the proud" (Proverbs 16:18-19, NIV).

Paul talks about his own thorn in 2 Corinthians 12:7 (NKJV). "And lest I should be exalted above the measure by the abundance of the revelations, a thorn in the flesh was given to me, a messenger of Satan to buffet me, lest I be exalted above measure."

We don't know what Paul's thorn was. I heard a pastor say it was good that we didn't know because we would definitely compare our thorn to his. We may believe ours was a worse thorn and feel beyond help, or we may think our thorn was not as bad as Paul's and feel superior. Either of these would take away from the message. The message was the purpose of the thorn. We all need something to remind us that we need God. Pastor Rich Wilkerson Jr. said, "Jesus is not my crutch. He's my stretcher."[9] As Christians, we don't just lean on Him, He carries us.

Paul asked God to take his thorn away. He asked three times, by the way. "Concerning this thing I pleaded with the Lord three times that it might depart from me" (2 Corinthians 12:8, NKJV).

Brother Paul, I pleaded way more than three times. There's nothing wrong with asking. It may seem like a shallow thing to ask for, however, the effect it's had on my life has been pervasive; it has affected me daily. You may think this thorn of mine is not so difficult to deal with, and I may think your thorn is superficial.

God can use anything that keeps us humble for our good and ultimately for His glory. He allows us to be pierced and sometimes stay pierced for a reason, and often it's tied into our purpose. Only the able hands of our Creator can transform pain into something good. He uses our brokenness and our wounds for a greater purpose and helps us heal in the meantime. The enemy deceives us when we believe we are strong enough in our own strength.

Paul comes to a conclusion about his thorn. "And He said to me, 'My grace is sufficient for you, for My strength is made perfect in weakness.' Therefore most gladly I will rather boast in my infirmities, that the power of Christ may rest upon me. Therefore I take pleasure in infirmities, in reproaches, in needs, in persecutions, in distresses, for Christ's sake. For when I am weak, then I am strong" (2 Corinthians 12:9-10, NKJV).

Whatever your thorn is, whether it's a physical ailment, a past mistake, an ongoing mental health issue, or something else, bring it to Your Father, like Elijah under the broom tree. State it plainly. It's got to be laid bare before the Great Physician. It's like a surgeon when he places drapes over a sick patient's body and exposes the area that needs repair. He takes that bright overhead light and adjusts it to shine directly over the place that needs work. God can do the same for you. He is your strength where you are weak.

Eventually I found a way to cover up the bald areas. There's a hair salon (many others similar to it have popped up) that is owned by a lovely lady named Bobbi. This salon specializes in helping women with hair loss. Bobbi uses a taping technique that allows me to walk around with hair. It's a miracle. I still know that I'm bald underneath it. I'm forever conscious of that. I'm not fooled one bit into thinking I've been transformed by something external. People are always impressed by what happened on the outside, but the real change is what happened on the inside. I'm grateful that God brought me to meet Bobbi via a Google search. I'm also thankful for a husband who loves me and thinks I'm beautiful as I am, hair or no hair. I had to accept myself first.

Technology has caught up. Now there are laser helmets, platelet-rich plasma (PRP) injections, scalp micropigmentation (SMP) treatments, and hair transplantations. I have options to try now that I didn't have when I was seventeen. Maybe one day I'll try one or all of them, but I'm not in a hurry anymore. I would walk around with my sparse hair *au naturel*, but it's such a distraction to people. They can't see me for my exposed scalp. I'm happy to share what I use to hide my balding areas with people when they ask, especially if it's a woman with alopecia. This girl, who was once ashamed when her head was pushed down and the thing she tried so hard to hide was exposed, will happily part the side of her hair to reveal her hair loss and show Bobbi's ingenious taping technique.

Chapter Eight

LET'S TALK ABOUT PURITY, BABY

When I didn't follow God's design for purity...

Even after I was saved, I spent the majority of my adult life believing that what the Bible said about sex before marriage was outdated. Sure it was practical back when people got married shortly after the onset of puberty, but I believed it was antiquated for present times. I was wrong. I didn't understand I was wrong by people telling me, but by God showing me.

Everything we do or say originates with a thought. To live right, we must think right. Our greatest battlefield against sin and temptation occurs in the mind. If our minds are not filled with God's truth, the enemy will pollute them with lies.

The enemy wants us to believe that if we follow Jesus we will suffer persecutions all the time. Let's clarify something. Suffering is a part of life, and there are seasons of it, some short and some long. This is true for any person living in this world because it is a fallen world, but when you suffer as a follower of Christ, you suffer with hope – sometimes just a sliver of it. That hope, even when it hangs by a thread, makes all the difference. One of the greatest testimonies to people who don't believe in Jesus is how a believer goes through tough times.

The enemy wants us to believe that if we follow Jesus, we will sacrifice all pleasure in our lives. I know from my own experience that my worst pain occurred when I followed my own desires and placed myself at the top of the altar to worship. When we follow Jesus, He is our reward, and so is the fruit of the Holy Spirit. That fruit brings peace and joy in times of trouble.

"For we do not wrestle against flesh and blood, but against principalities, against powers, against the rulers of the darkness of this age, against the spiritual hosts of wickedness in the heavenly places" (Ephesians 6:12, NKJV).

What does this verse mean? It means that we have an enemy, and he is the devil. It's hard for some people, perhaps most people, to believe that there are other dimensions and kingdoms around us that we cannot see. You cannot overcome the enemy in your life until you know that he is real. Charles Baudelaire is credited for saying, "The greatest trick the devil ever pulled was convincing the world that he didn't exist."[10] There are lies that become part of culture and are then integrated into beliefs, but they are not true. I think Satan sits back and laughs when we confuse lies for the truth.

"For such are false apostles, deceitful workers, transforming themselves into apostles of Christ. And no wonder! For Satan himself transforms himself into an angel of light. Therefore, it is no great thing if his ministers also transform themselves into ministers of righteousness, whose end will be according to their works" (2 Corinthians 11:13-14, NKJV).

So who was he and who is he? Satan was once an angel, and his angelic name was Lucifer, which translated in Latin means "light-bearer". In Luke 10:18 (NKJV), Jesus says, "I saw Satan fall like lightning from heaven." Lucifer was an angel designated to reflect the magnificence of God, but he began admiring his own beauty. He grew so enamored of himself that he became arrogant and desired to replace God.

Isaiah 14:12-15 (NKJV) describes Satan's rebellion:

> "How you are fallen from heaven,
> O Lucifer, son of the morning!
> How you are cut down to the ground,
> You who weakened the nations!
> For you have said in your heart:
> 'I will ascend into heaven,
> I will exalt my throne above the stars of God;
> I will also sit on the mount of the congregation
> On the farthest sides of the north;
> I will ascend above the heights of the clouds,
> I will be like the Most High.'

> Yet you shall be brought down to Sheol,
> To the lowest depths of the Pit."

The antithesis of Satan is not God, but rather the archangel Michael. As God is incomparable and has no equal, He cannot have an opposite. God vanquished Satan once and for all, and Jesus emerged victorious over him through the cross.

Satan's name translates to "accuser." Whom does he accuse?

He accuses us before God. Revelation 12:10-11 (NIV) says, "...the accuser of our brothers and sisters, who accuses them before our God day and night, has been hurled down. They triumphed over him by the blood of the Lamb and by the word of their testimony, and they did not love their lives to the death."

We are privy to an exchange between God and Satan in the book of Job. "Now there was a day when the sons of God came to present themselves before the Lord, and Satan also came among them. And the Lord said to Satan, 'From where do you come?' So Satan answered the Lord and said, 'From going to and fro on the earth and from walking back and forth on it.' Then the Lord said to Satan, 'Have you considered My servant Job, that there is none like him on the earth, a blameless and upright man, one who fears God and shuns evil?' So Satan answered the Lord and said, 'Does Job fear God for nothing? Have You not made a hedge around him, around his household, and around all that he has on every side? You have blessed the work of his hands, and his possessions have increased in the land. But now, stretch out Your hand and touch all that he has, and he will surely curse You to Your face!'" (Job 1:6-11, NKJV). Satan accused Job's character to God. He does the same with us before God. But when you are a true believer in Jesus, you are covered by the sacrifice He made on the cross.

Satan also accuses God to us by trying to discredit Him. What did Satan say about God to Eve in the Garden of Eden? He questioned her about what God really said to her and Adam about the tree. *Did He really say you would die if you ate from that tree, Eve? That's not what He actually meant, Eve.*

The pastor of a church I attended said that he pastored "a fatherless generation," that many of the families he pastored were led by single moms or families where it was the mom who brought the kids to church. The woman had taken over the spiritual leadership of the family, and it was never meant to be that way. Who was the man supposed to be? Let's go back again to the Garden of Eden.

We all know the story of the fall of mankind, but can I point out a detail to you?

"When the woman saw that the fruit of the tree was good for food and pleasing to the eye, and also desirable for gaining wisdom, she took some and ate it. She also gave some to her husband, who was with her, and he ate it. Then the eyes of both of them were opened, and they realized they were naked; so they sewed fig leaves together and made coverings for themselves" (Genesis 3:6-7, NIV).

What happened when Eve ate the fruit?

Nothing.

What happened when Adam, who was with her, ate the fruit?

Mankind fell.

From the beginning, since God joined man with the woman in the holy covenant of marriage, He has held the man as *spiritually accountable*. I would say based on what these verses in Genesis reveal, he is more accountable than the woman. I'm not saying that women are not accountable for themselves, because they surely are, but there was an additional spiritual accountability on Adam for the both of them that was not there on Eve.

I'm going to focus on this for few paragraphs because I think it has been taught incorrectly many times. This is something that happens when a man and woman join in marriage. The submission is mutual. I'm going to say it again. The submission is mutual and the same for husband and wife.

"The wife does not have authority of her own body but yields it to her husband. IN THE SAME WAY, the husband does not have authority over his own body but yields it to his wife" (1 Corinthians 7:4, NIV, emphasis added). When a man and woman join in the covenant of marriage, the man assumes a spiritual responsibility. It is an added responsibility over the spiritual climate of his family. He is accountable for encouraging them to pray and go to church. I have heard pastors talk about the man leading in a marriage and I believe the word "lead" has been taken out of context many times. It's a spiritual servant leadership, and the husband will have to answer to God for it one day.

Since that terrible day in Genesis, the story of the Bible lays out God's plan to bring man and woman back to Him, to redeem them through a savior. His name is Jesus Christ.

The Bible describes marriage, the relationship between the bridegroom and the bride, as analogous to the relationship of Jesus Christ (the bridegroom) to the church, (His bride). What did Jesus do for the church? He laid down His life willingly for her to live. Jesus was the all-powerful Son of God, and when He went to the cross, He had the ability to destroy every accuser who sent Him to His death. He could have commanded a multitude of angels from heaven to come to His rescue. Satan and all his demons probably taunted Him and thought of themselves as victorious. From being clothed in light and majesty to hanging naked on a wooden cross in shame, Jesus chose to carry guilt that wasn't His. He took that death sentence.

He did it for His church. He stayed up there in agony until His last breath was spent, until it was finished, and it was for her, His bride, His church because He loved her that much. And this is a picture of the marriage relationship. There isn't a woman in the world who wouldn't submit to such a love. Also, the greater beauty of it is that it is mutual and the same. As the church, we should be willing to lay down our lives for Him.

As women, we learn some lies about men. I've heard, "all men are selfish" and "all men are cheaters," and I have said these words myself. We as a society, as a culture, ever since the fall of man, have been taking accountability away from the man with statements like, "It's testosterone," or "he's a man," or "men are just biologically that way." But the Bible never said that men were more susceptible to sexual sin than women, or that it was impossible for men to overcome temptation. In fact, Hebrews 2:18 (NIV) says, "Because He Himself suffered when He was tempted, He is able to help those who are being tempted."

"No temptation has seized you except what is common to man. And God is faithful; *He will not let you be tempted beyond what you can bear*. But when you are tempted, He will also provide a way out so that you can stand up under it" (1 Corinthians 10:13, NIV, emphasis added). God may allow things to happen in your life that are more than you can bear *on your own*. He wants you to learn to lean on Him in your weakness. He does allow suffering and burdens that are too much to bear. It is in those times when we are so crushed that we can rely on His strength.

I've also heard the excuse that "men are visual". Moms of boys can teach their sons to avert their eyes. They may be more visual than women, but women are visual too. From an early age, we can teach our kids, boys and girls, that not all things, even those pleasing to the eye, are meant to be desired, pursued, and consumed.

I was taught in my teens that men couldn't love as deeply as women. That's another lie. Men and women are capable of the same depth of love. I've heard stories of men who laid down their life for a fellow soldier. I've seen how much a man can love his mother or his children. My own dad wouldn't hesitate to lay down his life for me. Men are capable of great love and loyalty, but I've had conversations with women who don't believe men are so able. So they've lowered their expectations, and then they encounter the wrong guys ready to meet those low expectations.

"Do not conform to the pattern of the world but be transformed by the renewing of your mind. Then you will be able to test and approve what God's will is – His good, *pleasing* and perfect will" (Romans 12:2, NIV, emphasis added).

The Word of God is the filter through which every thought should pass. We cannot learn to love His Word if we don't read it, esteem it, memorize it, and apply it to our lives.

If we abstain from sexual relationships, and I'm including everything from sexting to having intercourse with someone, it should come from genuine conviction that it's right for us to abstain, not that it's just the right thing to do. When I was in my early 20s before my first marriage, I abstained because in my culture and the home I grew up in, it was the right thing to do. Yet I found that when I abstained for that reason, I felt burned out and constantly struggling with desire. Abstinence was a burden. I couldn't sustain it.

After my divorce, for a few years, I didn't practice purity at all. Though I was not promiscuous or unsafe, my attitude was like, *forget this, I'm going to enjoy my life while I'm still alive.* But I learned the hard way that God didn't create me to live like that. I was lied to, manipulated, rejected, and disappointed, and I discovered that there were a lot of weirdos out there. It left me jaded and disillusioned, and I believed the worst in men. I ended up adding more emotional and spiritual injury to myself than I did going through a divorce.

I'm a little ashamed to say I had to be that uniquely broken to be open to what God wanted me to finally understand. God revealed truth to me about marriage and how the marital relationship was intended to be, starting from Adam and Eve and to Jesus and the church, the insights I shared at the start of this chapter. He gradually showed me how I had allowed the enemy to confuse me over my life. He convicted me to start praying for the men I knew, my friends' husbands, my ex-husband, my sons, and others. It then forced me to confront some lies I believed about men and what it meant to be in a relationship with a man. So it wasn't until after my divorce and after years of dating (not always in purity) that I uncovered all the lies I'd believed to be truth.

Then I finally made the choice to abstain, and the decision came from a genuine desire to honor God and from the deep-down-in-my-gut belief that sex outside of marriage ultimately brought me more grief than happiness. It was lightness in my heart and a joy to choose this, which could only be explained by the Holy Spirit in action. Much like when I became a Christian, acknowledged who Jesus was, and that I needed Him in my life as my Savior, instead of feeling burdened with rules and restrictions, I felt more freedom. When you obey out of love and not out of obligation or guilt, it's not necessarily a cakewalk, but it definitely is easier.

I know how difficult it is to practice purity when you don't have a genuine conviction for it. I'll give a simplified example. I have a friend who refuses to eat beef or pork, and this decision came after she toured a beef and pork manufacturing plant when she was in high school. What she saw, smelled, and learned there convinced her to never eat beef or pork again. She can't be tempted by the sight of a juicy, perfectly-grilled steak or the smell of bacon cooking. If the soup she orders tastes like it may have beef stock in it, she will return it. I couldn't see myself living that way. Sure, I could give up beef and pork for a limited time, but I don't have the desire to give them up for life. I also never had her experience, so I can't question her conviction. Indeed, if I had to face what she did that day at the processing plant, maybe I would change my mind too. You see, I went through enough pain, discomfort, and heartache dating outside of God's will that I chose wholeheartedly to practice purity. I've lived both ways, and I know which one is better.

I have another friend who was in and out of relationships with men and one day decided to not have sex before marriage because she believed it was the right thing to do. After about a year of abstaining, she started having an affair with a married man she worked with. When she explained why she made that choice, she said he made her feel valued at her job and as a person, that God hadn't brought the right guy/right one into her life after she stopped having sex for a year, and so she just went with it. She'd given God a year, and this married guy was who came along.

There are a couple of obvious issues here. First, God honors marriage. Period. The end. He's not going to bring a married person to you as a potential spouse no matter how unhappy that person's marriage is. Second, we can't put a time limit on God's plan for our lives. He doesn't move in the same time frame as ours or see time from the limited perspective that we have.

That conversation got me thinking about two other things. One I already mentioned was that the choice to abstain should come from heartfelt conviction. My friend felt the burden of abstinence, just like I had in my twenties, when it was just a rule to follow. The other idea I started to ponder was how we should "wait." The year that my friend stopped having sex was spent passively waiting. Yes, she attended church and exercised more and traveled, but she wasn't intentionally building the relationship that mattered most, the reason to abstain in the first place. She filled her life with distractions, which help for a short while but eventually cause burnout in the long term.

"Waiting" is an active process, not a passive one. It's not meant to be spent with distractions like working more, traveling more, or exercising more. Sure, you can enjoy those things as a single person, but the "waiting" is spent actively growing your relationship with Christ and moving closer to Him. How do we do this? We need to get personal with our God. Acknowledging His blessings daily. Spend time daily for prayer and take moments to praise Him. Be intentional in putting aside undistracted time to spend with Him. That's how you can learn to discern His voice better. Look into your heart regularly throughout the day. Check your thoughts throughout the day. The Word of God never talks about finding "The One" in terms of a spouse. Instead, it talks about being "the Right One".

Guard your heart when it comes to relationships with the opposite sex. There has to be a firm boundary, especially when we are in working relationships or friendships with married people of the opposite sex. The sexual act may happen spontaneously, which is why a lot of people who have affairs say, "it just happened." But the flirting, the thinking about the person, the time spent alone together for long hours, and the fantasizing are the things that create a pathway for the act to finally occur. Don't nurture those thoughts because they feed your feelings. There has to be a checkpoint where you don't allow that person to give you something that you should be getting from your Heavenly Father – your value and worth.

In I Corinthians 6:18 (NIV), Paul says to "flee from sexual immorality." He doesn't say turn away or walk away or be wary of but run. Isn't that what Joseph did with Potiphar's wife? He ran when she tried to tempt him into sleeping with her. So also, we should run from and not indulge the thoughts and the behaviors that will lead us down a path to this type of sin. It's hard to do. We can't do it on our own, only with God's help, and you have to admit you need His help to receive it.

When we have sex before marriage, we can confuse that physical and sexual chemistry as something more than what it is. It can fool us into thinking we have a genuine connection with the other person. We are more willing to overlook character flaws and make excuses for bad lifestyle and behavior choices. We are giving too much of ourselves too soon. Marriage is to be entered into with a sober mind.

Phillip Holmes is a blogger and finance coach, and he wrote an article on a site called desiringGod.org called "Drunk In Love: The Danger of Infatuation in Dating." I quote him as follows:

> Psychologists believe that dopamine is one of the key chemicals released in our brain that results in feelings of infatuation. Infatuation, as defined by the Oxford Dictionary, is an intense but short-lived passion or admiration for someone or something. It becomes dangerous when it's confused with the love it takes to make a marriage last.
>
> Serial daters are dopamine addicts. They date for about six months, enjoy the euphoric experience that a new relationship brings, and then break up when real life begins and infatuation ends. They do this over and over again. Serial daters generally have a hard time once they decide to marry because committing to one man or one woman means giving up access to the experience they crave. They lived life drunk on dopamine, and now they've made a commitment that keeps them from that high.

When you compare the effects of drunkenness to those of infatuation, you find a lot of similarities. Drunkenness causes irrational behavior (Genesis 9:20–22), suppresses our conscience (Genesis 9:24–25), and impairs our ability to make good judgment (Proverbs 31:4–5). The same is true with infatuation and lust. Those driven by their passions and lusts are usually irrational, go against what their conscience says is right and wrong, and make terrible decisions that could negatively affect the rest of their lives.[11]

Once I had accepted God's Word as truth and admitted that I was done with doing things my way and wanted to follow His design, I asked God for confirmation about waiting until marriage to have sex. I think God likes it when we ask Him to confirm for us what we've read in His Word. He generously gave me confirmations through other people's testimonies. Random conversations about couples that waited would come up with friends or in articles I read. He brought the confirmation in exactly the way I needed but not in the way I expected, which I've found is often how God works. I would trust Him daily to teach me how to stay pure. He showed me what I should avoid watching for too long, which thoughts led to longing, and so I learned to redirect my thinking.

I also learned to trust Him through this process. Soon I was convinced the right person would come at the right time, and it would not require any manipulation of circumstances on my part. I was focused on becoming the right person for whoever was right for me. If I say I trust God, then I should definitely trust Him with something as important as with whom I spend the rest of my life, and if marriage was not His plan for me, I accepted that as well.

Marriage is not the destiny of every single person on this planet. You can live a fulfilling, joyful life, full of purpose as a single. When I was single and practicing purity, I felt like I could have continued that way for the rest of my life. I didn't mind being a third or fifth wheel when I went out with married couples. I didn't see them as happier or more fulfilled than me. In fact, they often seemed more stressed, preoccupied, and over-scheduled. The more people are intimately entwined in your life, the more responsibility and accountability you have, and the more your personal time is taken away. So marriage, just like parenthood, is not for everybody, and that's okay.

Chapter Nine

REJECTION

When I've been rejected…

Everyone has faced rejection at some point in his or her life. Since it's inevitable in life, I prefer rejection to be clear and direct. Don't string me along or give me false hope. If it's not going to happen, then say it. Make it a clean wound. That doesn't mean I like rejection. It is a wound that can cut deeply.

After my divorce, when I spent about two years as a single woman, not interested in anyone, not dating anyone, I walked in purity. I was on automatic pilot. It was easy. I loved God, and I lived my life with joy, the cherished daughter of the King of Kings. He banished the loneliness that had been a dark lurking shadow over me since childhood. I had a Father in heaven that protected me, provided for me, and spoke love into my heart. I could have lived happily forever single. The last thing I needed was to notice a man at my church, but that is exactly what happened.

He was single and handsome, a few years younger than me, with a warm smile that reached his blue eyes. People I knew at church admired and respected him and told me he was a good guy. When he would smile at me, well, I felt butterflies for the first time in years. It was nice to know that I could experience those feelings again, but at the same time, I was annoyed that those feelings were happening. A struggle with my past resurfaced, and my peace was challenged.

My church was my sanctuary. There was no one I wanted to avoid there. I was welcomed as family, and I belonged there. I tried to ignore him and not notice him, but I couldn't help it. I wanted to get to know him, however, I also feared that if anything happened between him and me, and it didn't work out, then that would ruin the church, my safe place, for me.

I felt paralyzed by memories of rejection, some from decades ago. The recollection of my crushed hopes and dreams rendered me helpless. The enemy was quick to remind me about all of my past rejections.

I would remember every insult that had been thrown my way over the past forty years: You're too dark. You're too fat. Your hair is thinning. He's too good-looking for you. He's outgoing and won't like when you are quiet. If looking at him gives you butterflies, then he will surely reject you. You'll never get the guy that makes you feel that way. This is your history that is bound to repeat itself in an endless cycle.

The verse that helped me was, "I have loved you with an everlasting love. I have drawn you with unfailing kindness" (Jeremiah 31:3, NIV).

God's words there reminded me that regardless of who might reject me, whether it's my friendship or something more, Jesus has never rejected me, even during the years of my life when I rejected Him. He had chosen me. I was already loved perfectly as a child of God.

I played worship music to get through this struggle. Hillsong Worship's song, *Jesus I Need You*, was on repeat. When I heard the voice of my past that disqualified me, I would try to magnify my God. He would speak to my heart and soothe my re-opened wounds with words like, "I have not disqualified you" and "I have not rejected you." Then "this grace-bought heart" would remember that His "loving kindness has never failed me." So whenever you hear that disqualifying voice, remember "Christ before me" and "Christ behind me."

Ultimately, after many tears and moments when my stomach was twisting into knots, I resolved to just hope for friendship, and it was my daily prayer that I not imagine the blue-eyed man at my church as anything more. Again there was that concept of "capturing every thought and making it obedient to Christ." I didn't place an expectation of anything more, and my peace was restored. Every time that anxiety welled up inside me, I would lay it at the foot of the cross, intentionally, desperately. It became a reflex, then eventually a habit and easier with time.

Author Sharon Jaynes who writes for an email devotional called "Girlfriends in God" (girlfriendsingod.com) said, "What the devil really wants to do is to steal your confidence, and the best time to rob you blind is during a season of disappointment."[12] So stop giving the enemy a foothold in your thought life. "For God has not given us a spirit of fear, but of power and of love and of a sound mind" (2 Timothy 1:7, NKJV).

There are some rejections that you kind of expect and are braced for, and some that still sting, no matter how much mental prep you've done. When I considered switching careers after fifteen years of practicing medicine, I thought I was a great candidate. I had a doctorate, years of leadership experience, and excellent time management and organizational skills. Then I was rejected for job after job, and after the sixteenth rejection in a row, I began to feel discouraged. One week I had three rejections and two of them were on a Friday. My head felt heavy as I awoke Saturday morning. My soul was weary. I wondered if everything I had done up to that point in life had been pointless. How was I so unqualified with all my education and experience?

Unqualified, rejected, worthless.

The derogatory adjectives to describe myself kept circling in my brain like vultures. I felt so small. I crawled out of bed that Saturday morning, but I didn't have the luxury of time for wallowing in self-pity. I had to take my son to a volunteer event. The dog had a much-needed grooming appointment. I needed to make meals for my family. There were piles of laundry to wash, dry, and sort. Throughout the day, the discouragement hung on me like a weight. My smile didn't reach my eyes, and words of self-condemnation resounded in my mind every spare moment.

It's funny how past rejections, the ones I thought I'd gotten over, resurfaced. I have a strong memory of events. Someone once told me I had a memory like an elephant, stretching past decades. It was fine for when I was studying for an exam, but it wasn't so great when I would relive past rejections and the pain I felt from them as if they were happening in real time. That day the memories came back like an avalanche.

That Saturday sucked rocks. But then there was Sunday.

I had time for some solitude in the morning before everyone else woke up, time on my knees to be under that broom tree figuratively. Deeply humbled and with my soul troubled, I began to write in my prayer journal. I wanted to tell God about how terrible I felt, about all the awful memories that kept replaying in my mind, rehashing those events He had already dealt with for me. Before I put a word down on paper, God stopped me. I checked the You Version Bible app verse of the day.

"And every creature which is in heaven and on the earth and under the earth and such as are in the sea, and all that are in them, I heard saying:

'Blessing and honor and glory and power

Be to Him who sits on the throne,

And to the Lamb, forever and ever!'" (Revelation 5:13, NKJV).

Praise Me, He whispered to my heart.

I've learned to obey. A song came to mind to help me, one that I'd not listened to for years, *When the Stars Burn Down* by Phillips, Craig & Dean. The chorus comes from that verse in Revelation, "blessing and honor and glory and power forever to our God."

As I listened to the words and focused on how one day every living thing would bow down to the majesty of the one Righteous King, my problems diminished. They didn't vanish. I hadn't received a job offer, but I had hope again. That is our greatest witness as believers, to have hope that makes no sense and joy that is ludicrous, given our circumstances. It was like God applied a healing balm over the wounds of rejection.

He reminded me that one of His names is El Roi.

And I remembered Hagar's story. Hagar was the Egyptian servant of Sarai (later Sarah). When Sarai couldn't have any children, she gave Hagar to Abram (later Abraham) so that he could have children through her. But when Hagar became pregnant, there was some mean-girl, sister-wife strife between them, and Hagar ran away.

While Hagar was pregnant and alone in the wilderness, God spoke to her. He instructed her to go back to Sarai and gave her news that her son would have many descendants. "'...Because the Lord has heard your affliction'" (Genesis 16:11, NKJV). That's what the angel of the Lord reassured her; she didn't go unnoticed. She wasn't the one that the nation of Israel would come from, but neither was she rejected nor an outcast.

"Then she called the name of the Lord who spoke to her, You-Are-the-God-Who-Sees; for she said, 'Have I also here seen Him who sees me?' Therefore the well was called Beer Lahai Roi..." (Genesis 16:13-14, NKJV). The name Beer Lahai Roi means "Well of the One Who Lives and Sees Me."

El Roi was one of God's names, and it meant "the God who sees me." In the original Hebrew, "Ro'iy" translated into shepherd, as someone who was seeing or looking.

God was reminding me that He sees every rejection. He notices every time you and I are marginalized, forgotten, invisible, and rejected; He let me know that He was Lord over all of it, for me and for you.

"And we know that all things work together for good to those who love God, to those who are called according to His purpose" (Romans 8: 28, NKJV).

That's one of my favorite verses in the Bible. It's an assurance that even the rejections in your life can be worked out for good because it is El Roi who is in charge. He's not taken by surprise, though you and I may be. He sees the beginning from the end, and He is already at the end ready to hold you. Soren Kierkegaard, Danish theologian, poet, critic, and philosopher (1813-1855) said, "Life can only be understood backwards, but it must be lived forwards."[13] Most of the time we won't see the good without hindsight, whether that be on earth or once we get to heaven, but one day, He will surely let us see what He saw.

Chapter Ten

DO NOT MARK YOUR PRECIOUS SKIN

When I injured myself to feel better…

These were the words that God spoke to my spirit when I was talking with a patient of mine who was cutting herself. He said, "My child, do not mark your precious skin."

I wish I'd had someone to tell me that when I was a thirteen-year-old in middle school, before I took a razor blade and cut lines over my wrists. This was back in the late 1980s when no one really talked about cutting. It wasn't a fad, and there was no posting about it. This was pre-social media, and it was something that I hid. At the time, I didn't understand why I did it, but I knew it was probably shameful and not something to share with other people, least of all my conservative, traditional Indian family. I knew it somehow made me feel better, like a relief, a flood of painful emotion expelled in the physical aching of my skin.

It's a form of self-injury. In the scientific community, there is some dispute and inconsistent findings regarding why people engage in self-injury. Several neurobiological systems may be involved. The self-injury can make a person "feel" again after experiencing numbness or dullness in emotions following a traumatic experience. Some find it a way to express personal pain, or it may feel like a way to have control over it.

Why do people cut themselves? Often times, it is not to kill themselves, though sometimes when the device they use is in their hands, the thought does cross their mind, *What if I did it deeper this time? What if I did it so deep that I bled out and died?* The act of inflicting pain on oneself brings a relaxing feeling. To manifest the emotional and spiritual pain in a physical palpable form offers comfort, but that relief is temporary, and I think it is a trick of the enemy, as are most temporary fixes.

God was aware that I would confront hardships in this world, but He gave His word that any affliction I encountered would never take me away from His love.

Remember that God delights in you. The Bible says, "The Lord your God is with you, He is mighty to save. He will take great delight in you, He will quiet you with His love, He will rejoice over you with singing" (Zephaniah 3:17, NIV).

Sometimes that's been difficult for me to grasp. Why was it so hard for me sometimes to believe it in my bones? I had a conversation with God about this during one of my seasons under the broom tree. I thought prayerfully about what it meant to delight in someone you love.

An image immediately came to mind of my younger son playing with dinosaur toys. It is a cherished memory. I was reading a book on the couch, and I heard him talking, only he was three years old with some speech delay, so some of what he said was hard to understand. With a T-Rex in one hand and an allosaurus (I think) in the other, he was pretending that one was talking to the other. Then they would fight, which was basically him colliding them together and making crashing sounds. I watched him with an emotion in my heart that I could only describe as delight. I was delighting in him and his sweet, childlike, playful exuberance. How does God delight in me? The same way I delighted in my son in that moment, but because He's God, that delight is greater and more intense.

The next story is a difficult one for me to share, because in my culture, just like cutting, it's something we don't talk about, but I'm choosing to be candid and transparent. God has convinced me that there is at least one hurting heart that will read the words He's penned through me and find healing.

I wrote a suicide note when I was in middle school. My teenage mind had contemplated all the reasons why I should not exist. I was a malformed, misshapen, unlovable person. I shouldn't have been born. I was surely a mistake, and it was time for me to take corrective action. I was serious about my decision. I had a plan in place.

I gave the note to the only friend I had at the time. I wasn't dramatic about it or tearful. The letter was my goodbye and all of my "whys". It scared my friend, and she gave it to the school nurse. The nurse then called me to her office during class and talked with me. I remember feeling surprised, a little offended, a little betrayed, and then really, really scared that she was going to tell my parents. She asked me to promise that I wasn't going to go through with it. She made me give her a verbal contract of safety. So I promised her. I don't know that this technique works on every kid, but it did on me because my word still meant something. The nurse also reminded me that even if I believed that no one loved me, my friend proved that belief to be false; she loved me enough to interrupt my plans and risk losing my friendship. My life mattered to her.

Never hesitate to interrupt someone if your gut tells you something is up. They may be contemplating ending their life. Whether you feel like you should send an encouraging text, invite a person to a meal or to coffee, whatever nudges your intuition gives you, please follow up. That young girl saved my life. Kids need just one person to believe in them, to stand up for them, to love them. They don't need a hundred partially invested followers. They need the one.

After I gave my heart to Jesus at a Bible study in college, I never had the desire to cut again or to end my life. It left me. That is how I know Jesus is real. I know He is the real deal because I lived out the change in me after accepting Him as God. I didn't become a perfect person. I'm still not a perfect person, nor do I hope to achieve such a state while I'm here on this earth. There was a tremendous, life-long journey that awaited me after making the decision to believe that He is who He says He is in His Word. That journey is ongoing, even as I write this sentence and long after I finish penning it, but I go through the journey differently than before. I live this life with a different perspective, with a hope and with a respect for the life He gave me that I didn't have before I recognized Him as God.

I still struggle with anxiety. There are days when my anxiety is so intense – much like our friend Elijah – that it reacquaints me with the loneliness and isolation I felt as a teenager. Those same incessant phrases repeat in my head in such times like they did when I was a teen, and they threaten to take me into what I call the dark downward spiral.

"You're the only one."

"There's no one to trust with this."

"There's no one to talk to about it."

"Let me play out for you how much worse this can get."

It's at that point God taught me to say, "Stop! You can go no further," and with my eyes closed, I remind my treacherous mind that God sees me and delights in me because I am someone He loves.

Then comes redirection; He's already told me what to think about instead:

Whatever is true.

Whatever is noble.

Whatever is right.

Whatever is pure.

Whatever is lovely.

Whatever is admirable.

Anything excellent or praiseworthy.

Think about such things.

That's Philippians 4:8 and practicing this rewires a new pathway in my mind, something good for the neurons to fire about, and the dark spiral disintegrates.

Chapter Eleven

GETTING OVER THE GUY

When I've held onto something too tightly that was never meant for me to begin with...

During a divorce, you may be one of two things, emotionally vulnerable or emotionally unavailable. A lot of us who go through that agonizing process will shut ourselves down, steeling ourselves against more pain. We just don't want to deal with more than what we already have on our plates. I did that for a while, but then something unexpected happened.

Remember when I said earlier to be careful whom you find, who seems to pop into your life, when your expectations are diminished, when your thoughts of yourself are low? Have caution of whom you let into your circle and into your weary heart. Be wary of the words, the information fed to you, and the thoughts that those words create in your mind. This is especially true for anyone going through a divorce.

When my marriage ended, and before I decided to live in purity, I became friends with a single guy. He was an incredibly attractive and charismatic man I had known of for a while. We had multiple mutual friends, but I'd never really gotten to know him personally. Through having conversations with him and becoming friends with him, I found myself emotionally open, not just to anyone, but specifically to him. I looked forward to the texts and phone calls. I was able to say so much with such freedom and without any fear of being judged. I went from being emotionally unavailable to incredibly vulnerable, and it felt like a punch to the gut. I was falling for him before I had fully healed from what I had gone through.

It seemed as if he liked me in that way, too, so I suggested we pursue this, not jumping in but going slowly.

And he rejected me.

I didn't have the emotional strength to deal with it. I left God out of the situation and tried to handle it on my own. I made a profile on a dating website and became a serial dater, something I'd never done in my entire adult life. I compartmentalized the pain of his rejection and stuffed it deep down where I didn't have to face it. When it would rear its ugly head, I would just keep burying it. That box of pain was like poorly-contained toxic waste buried under a house. It was leaking out and making the inhabitant of that house (me) sick. Somehow, like an emotional masochist, I couldn't completely stop myself from thinking about him. He had gotten under my skin like no one had ever done before, and I couldn't displace or replace him. Believe me, I tried! I wasn't wired to be a player. That's not how God made me. It didn't matter how many guys said I was beautiful or how many people liked my selfies. At the core, I felt rejected and was trying to compensate. Toxic waste must be removed and processed appropriately, or its poison will continue to seep out.

I described in a previous chapter how I finally chose to walk in purity. That came years later. Part of the process of choosing purity was dealing with this past hurt and checking the state of my heart. Trying to live more in that damaged heart was an uncomfortable but necessary process. It's very easy for me to live in my head, with my logic and reason and ability to shut out unpleasant events and box up pain.

Then the news came that I had dreaded.

He was getting married.

I wasn't ready for him to marry. I didn't want to have these feelings for a married man. I didn't have closure.

I knew how to let someone go. I knew how to get past things. I had to get over a ten-year marriage so why couldn't I get over this guy? I believed I should be good at this "letting go and moving on" business by now. Instead, I was stuck in a place where I didn't believe I could care as strongly and deeply again. I couldn't connect emotionally on that level again. It was like that part of my heart that could fully love a man was burned out and ruined.

It brought me to my knees under the broom tree.

I can't go on like this, Jesus. Help me confront it.

I felt the burden of his rejection like a crushing weight on my chest. I relived it fresh. I let myself feel it, and if I hadn't had Jesus holding me up, I would have surely crumbled from the pain. I wished I hadn't felt that depth of emotion for someone.

I believed in my bones that this man was above me, out of my league. I put him up there on that pedestal, so his rejection validated a dark, negative belief I had about myself. I was not worthy, not good enough, overly flawed, especially in my physical appearance. I didn't look like his type. I disqualified myself. It was my own voice in my head speaking out the disqualification, not his. He never told me why he rejected me, and I definitely didn't ask.

So I prayed and prayed but made little progress. I couldn't push past this. I had joined a Lifegroup around that time, and after several meetings, I gathered the courage to admit my situation. That night, the wonderful ladies in my Lifegroup prayed for me. When they did that, I finally had the breakthrough. Can I just tell you that Lifegroups are great? Find a group of believers through your church that you can do life with. When we pray together, awesome things happen.

Chains are broken. Shame is cast out, and prayers are answered.

I prayed on my own after my friends had prayed for me, and I felt the difference. Three realizations came to me about this guy's rejection of me:

1) I had unforgiveness toward him in my heart. I still wanted an apology and/or explanation for what happened. Why exactly did he reject me? I already had a hunch that there was unforgiveness. I had to let that go, and I knew I could. I was already working on that part, but after I shared my story with my Lifegroup, I was surprised to find that shame and embarrassment lost their power. I didn't realize they were there, too. I was used to being in control of myself, and I was ashamed of how uncontrolled I was with this person.

2) God told me that it was okay to look at his picture. I considered looking at his picture as something forbidden for years. I reasoned that if I avoided looking at him, then that would help me get over him. Instead, it gave him more of an unattainable quality and a greater appeal. So God said, "Look at him." Then He put me in check and He said, "Wait, stop lusting at his picture. Check your heart. Look at him with Me. I'm right here. It's okay to feel. And it's okay to cry when you look at him. Not a tear is wasted in My presence. I see the pain

you can't explain to anyone with words. You don't have to explain it to Me. Lay that pain at My feet. I already see it, but I want you to willingly share that pain with Me." So, like a troll, I looked at the pictures on his social media, the ones that destroyed me. However, I looked at them with the right heart and a sober mind, and I felt the grip of this infatuation loosen.

3) I'd been holding onto something tightly in my fist. I wasn't letting it go. I wouldn't relax my grip to look at it so I didn't understand what it was. This was the thing keeping me the most stuck. It was the possibility of a future with him (you can insert your own person or desire here). This was the hope that refused to die, that we would come to a place in our lives someday in the future, just like we did after years of knowing of each other and finally meeting. That future meeting would be the right place, the right time. I saw him as someone who tied my past, present, and future together like he was someone already known to me. That was always one of his biggest appeals. I had known of him for half my life, and when I got to know him better one-on-one, with emotional intimacy, it was a wonderful heart and mind connection. So I made a tight fist, saying I was holding the possibility of a future with him in there, and I opened my hand and

released it to my heavenly Father. God spoke to my heart, "Putting that hope in Me will feel like an unnatural exercise for a while, but every time you voluntarily and purposefully and mindfully do, it will feel right. The pain doesn't suddenly stop here, but let Me make it better with time. You are in a habit of imagining a future with him, and you will need to take those thoughts captive and bring them before Me."

Second Corinthians 10:5 (NIV) says, "We demolish arguments and every pretension that sets itself up against the knowledge of God, and we take captive every thought to make it obedient to Christ." I had to capture those thoughts and reject them when they did not line up with Christ's words.

Pastor Steven Furtick said, "God cannot heal what you hide."[14] Now, keep in mind that God sees it because nothing is hidden from Him, but He wants you to relax that grip, open that hand, and voluntarily and purposefully reveal it. Surrender it.

God wants you to give that hope to Him. Entrust Him with it. Your hope doesn't have to die. Let God be your future. Hope will thrive in Him. You may have to practice this like I did. I had been holding on so hard, keeping that hope where I thought it should be, even doing so subconsciously, not realizing it was misplaced.

Author Sharon Jaynes wrote:

But when we are wounded emotionally, it's not quite that straightforward. We can't see the wound, so it often goes unattended, festering and spreading infection into our thoughts and relationships. Time does not heal all wounds, especially wounds of the heart. They may lie dormant for a season, but triggers poke them with the hot iron of remembrance that lets us know they're still there. Forgiveness begins with a decision, but there is also a process that follows. The mind and emotions don't always move in tandem. Emotions tend to lag behind. Even when we make a sincere decision to forgive, it might take a while for our emotions to catch up. [15]

Keep in mind also that when you bury the box full of the hurts from past relationships, it has a way of resurfacing when you try to start a relationship with someone new. And that's not fair to that new someone or to that new relationship that deserves a clean start.

This was how I healed from a heart wound that held me hostage for years. I've heard stories from friends about people in their lives with whom there were emotional ties, romantic ties, they could never completely get over. So I would encourage you to dig deep and see if there's anyone that has his or her hooks in you. Maybe it's time to finally let that person go, once and for all.

Chapter Twelve

MOMS AND VIRTUES

When I couldn't forgive…

There was a time in my life when I was unable to forgive someone close to me who raised me but had done me wrong. That unforgiveness inside me, buried in a porous box, seeped bitterness into my life. I didn't recognize its negative effect on me until I found myself in a dark place, forced to finally face my hurt and anger. It was a broom tree moment, and God met me there.

Someone once told me that all moms love their children unconditionally. I've never believed that as an absolute truth. I'd practiced in pediatrics long enough to see all types of moms. I'd seen moms whose unhealthy co-dependent relationships with their children crippled them as adults. I'd seen mothers who lost their children because they prostituted them for drugs. I'd also seen great moms who did their best and raised kind, caring humans. I came to a conclusion that the greatest gift any mom can give her child is to do her utmost to be a healthy person, mentally, spiritually, physically, and emotionally.

What happens when a mom is mentally unwell and doesn't seek help? Moms are the emotional thermostats for their homes. When Mom is not in a good place, everyone feels it.

Mental illness in my culture is taboo. No one wants to talk about it. It's only the current generation, my generation, that is starting to open up about mental health, but I know what I say in this chapter will rub a lot of people in my culture the wrong way.

I grew up with a mom with undiagnosed mental illness. I could never talk about it with anyone because it was an uneasy conversation. Anytime I would try to talk about it with Indian people, they would shrug it off and marginalize what I was trying to convey. The topic made them visibly uncomfortable. But our parents are human too, just like us. Why is it shameful when they or any of us struggle with something?

Based on what I've learned of my mom's history and from a lifetime of daily interactions with her, my suspicion was that she had borderline personality disorder. She didn't have a typical childhood. Hers was a painful one discolored by abandonment and poverty.

Borderline personality disorder (BPD) is fairly common with around 3 million cases in the US per year. According to the American Psychiatric Association, BPD is "a pervasive pattern of instability of interpersonal relationships, self-image, and affects, and marked impulsivity, beginning in early adulthood and present in a variety of contexts."

What's it like when your mom has borderline personality disorder?

She will regularly say things like, "I'm going to kill myself if you don't do ___." Or she may say, "I'm going to leave you if you do ___." This is not a one time or two-time exclamation, it is said often. She frequently threatens her children with abandonment in an effort to manipulate them. She gives ultimatums to get her way. She encourages or creates conflict so she can experience her own emotional catharsis. She will have her child believing that they are best friends, but once her child makes a mistake, she will treat that child as if he or she has betrayed her. She brandishes closeness to her like a weapon and a commodity to be earned. In her mind, even the imagined slight is a mark against you. She keeps score.

She'll read your diary or journal if you have one, and to get you to do what she wants, she'll threaten to tell people what you wrote. She'll look through your things to find if you're hiding something from her. No secret should be trusted with her. She's ready to betray you as punishment for any perceived offense.

The mom with borderline personality disorder cuts off her love as a punishment. She'll ignore you. She'll walk out of a room when you walk into it to let you know that you've wronged her in some way. She will persist until you pursue her on your knees, apologizing and asking for forgiveness, when most of the time you're not even sure what you did wrong. When she has decided that you're back on good terms with her, she's a dream come true – loving, kind, and caring. She'll make your favorite foods and suddenly want to be around you and talk about life. You're either obsidian black or snow white. For her there are no shades of gray in you.

There are days you come home from school, and she's sitting on the ground, practically catatonic. She refuses to speak. She's completely withdrawn into herself and won't communicate. Then, suddenly, her mood will shift, and she's very happy for no apparent reason, but you know it won't last.

You are constantly tiptoeing; you never know when she'll choose to take her love and affection away because of something you do wrong, whether the offense is real or contrived. Once she feels you have suffered enough or shown sufficient remorse, she'll go back to being loving again… until next time… and there's always a next time.

Perhaps the worst outcome I've seen from moms with BPD is that they often create a child who grows up to be the same. Her child may cut her off without a second glance back in her direction, and that child will do the same in his or her other relationships as well.

As a young person, I allowed my mom's mood to affect my mood. I didn't realize or understand what was going on with her. I just learned how to cope with it and survive. So I didn't grow up holding a grudge against her. In fact, I loved her like any kid loves their mom. *What was wrong with me*, I wondered, *that she didn't always love me back?*

After I had my first son at the age of thirty, I realized what it meant to love a child as a mother. Then it hit me like a freight train, the things my mom had done to my sister and me our whole lives, and I was filled with rage against her. I saw the damage, the aftermath that had overflowed into both of our lives, and I just couldn't forgive her.

Marianne Williamson said, "Unforgiveness is like drinking poison yourself and waiting for the other person to die." [16] It will make you bitter and destroy your heart. When you forgive someone, it doesn't excuse his or her behavior, and you shouldn't wait for them to apologize before you do it, because the apology may never come.

Forgiveness isn't the same thing as trust. Just because you forgive someone doesn't mean you have to trust him or her. If someone sexually abused you as a child, it doesn't mean you entrust your own child to that person, as if the abuse never happened. It doesn't mean you have to continue in a close relationship with that person. It doesn't mean you stay in an abusive relationship and just allow someone to continue abusing you. You create a healthy distance and appropriate boundaries. Trust has to be earned, and there will be people you forgive who will never earn back trust.

Jesus was the most forgiving being to walk the earth. He forgave everyone, even while they nailed Him to the cross. But the Bible tells us that He didn't trust everyone. John 2:23-24 (NIV) says, "Now while He was in Jerusalem at the Passover Festival, many people saw the signs He was performing and believed in His name. But Jesus would not entrust Himself to them, for He knew all people. He did not need testimony about mankind, for He knew what was in each person."

We forgive because God has forgiven us for so much. I think it's the hardest thing to master as a Christian, but we are never more Christ-like than when we forgive someone who doesn't deserve it. I find it extremely difficult at times, and it's something I can't do without the help of the Holy Spirit. Forgiveness rarely happens instantly, it builds over time and has to be intentional. One way I know I'm there is if I can replay the event in my mind without the pain or the anger.

Even when I understood how important forgiveness was, I still struggled to forgive my mother. I looked back at my childhood years with contempt for her. In social situations, I would say mean, digging remarks to her. That was how I acted as a thirty-something year old woman. I would tell people that it was my dad who raised me. I would say that I was like him, not like her. There is some truth in those statements. I do take after my dad in a lot of ways, and he is the parent who took an interest in my education and what I was accomplishing with my life. Out of spite, I would deny my mom's hand in raising me. I couldn't relate to women who said their mom was their best friend. I would think, *wow, they know nothing about life.*

I couldn't break the unforgiveness, and it embittered me. It would bring me to my knees in seething anger. I would imagine ways to hurt her and make her feel my pain. Perhaps you find yourself caught in a similar trap of thoughts, not necessarily against your mother, but against someone else who hurt you deeply and repeatedly for a long period of your life. Besides, it wasn't like she'd changed. She was still using the same tactics to manipulate me as an adult. She was still gossiping about me to her friends. It's so hard to forgive when the person still does the very thing that you are trying to forgive them for.

It was in the Lifegroup I mentioned previously that I finally made progress. We were reading the book, *Fervent* by Priscilla Shirer[17]. Two things I would like to recommend here: first, and again I say, join a Lifegroup because it's in the intimacy of a small group where you will experience tremendous change in your daily walk with Christ. Second, read *Fervent* because it's awesome.

The group of six exceptional women that I was privileged to be a part of was going over the chapter in *Fervent* about our pasts, and we started talking about our moms. I opened up about something that I had previously been ashamed to discuss with anyone, and that was about the emotional abuse I experienced with my mom and how loving her was always difficult because it was as if she couldn't give or receive love in any genuine way. One of the women shared how she and her sister were subjected to physical and emotional abuse from their mom and how the abuse was still ongoing into their adulthood. Then she said something that floored me: "Moms teach us virtues."

My response was that I thought my mom taught me virtues by demonstrating how not to be. My friend repeated, "Moms teach us virtues." God wouldn't let me forget those words of wisdom. He spoke to my heart after our discussion to think about that statement a little more, to look a little deeper into my childhood but from a different perspective. So I did. This is what I felt impressed upon me.

My friend came out of *all* that painful childhood and was able to say, "Moms teach us virtues." She was able to make that statement even when the abuse was continuing in her life in that relationship with mom. How could I come to that point? I wanted to, but didn't know how.

This is what God pressed onto my heart: Forgive her mistakes and whatever mess she makes. Have an endless supply of forgiveness for her because you will need it. You do not fully understand the pain of your mother's childhood. She grew up in a time when there was no help for someone in her situation. There was no therapy in India, and she was taught that to seek it out was something to be ashamed of. Understand that she raised you and loved you in the capacity that her psyche allowed. She could do no more. She believed that just being alive in your life was more than enough because it was more than she'd had from her mom. You don't know how many times she may have come to ending her own life, but then stopped when she thought of you being left motherless, like she was.

Understand that you weren't shown a quality example of how to be a wife, of how to be a mother, and know that you cannot mimic her or follow that example. She modeled certain bad behaviors for years, and you will be tempted to adopt those as your own. The unhealthy behaviors don't ever have to be yours, but remember that she did some good things, too. Don't you always make sure your sons get a hot meal every evening for their dinner? Who did you learn that from? The same mother who wronged you. You can choose to do the good. If you don't forgive her, it will change you into a mother you don't want to be.

I can be an even better mother by choosing to love the way Jesus loves. Jesus is the best example of how to be a good parent. He wasn't a parent, but He loved like a good one.

God always provides. He gives us what we need but not always in the way we expect. I wanted a magical "poof" and voilà, I've suddenly achieved forgiveness. The emotions lag behind but will catch up to the decision eventually if we are earnest and persistent in seeking His will and His wisdom about the situation.

We're meant to carry burdens for a while to learn something from them regarding our purpose, but we are not meant to hold onto those burdens forever. At some point we are meant to let go. My friend chose to love her mom despite the hurt and the difficulty. I also had a choice to love my mom although she's hard for me to love. I could choose to not cut her out of my life, and in making these choices, I realized how my mother taught me virtues.

What happens to us when we choose to love someone close to us who has offended us? It teaches us to love more unselfishly. I looked back at my childhood with a different perspective. I saw the times I pursued her and was patient with her when she was in one of her moods. I saw the times, as a child, when I was able to respond to her snapping at me with kindness, never cursing her, even as a teenager. I never shut her out as a child, even when she shut me out. I was taught kindness and patience. She didn't model it, but she taught me how to be a better person. Love, kindness, patience... all virtues. So I made a choice to put those virtues to use and stop being bitter. I admit I still love my mom imperfectly, but I don't hold onto the past grudges like I did.

I needed to be free of that heart pain. Mark Batterson said, "The circumstances we ask God to change are often the circumstances God is using to change us." [18] I couldn't redo my past. I couldn't wish my childhood into some beautiful fairytale, but I could allow forgiveness to transform my mind and, therefore, my present and my future.

I allowed forgiveness to unburden me, and suddenly I could see better why God put my mom in my life. I could see better how it changed me. Sure it brought me pain. There was emotional abuse in my life because of that relationship, but I have the Spirit-driven ability and authority as a daughter of an Almighty undefeated God to move past what I need to move past and battle what I need to battle. We are meant to overcome and be transformed in the act of overcoming into a character that is more like our Savior's. What an amazing God we have who can change our perspective on what we thought was a burden! It just took a few words of truth from a friend and the power of the Holy Spirit.

"God sees the beginning from the end." [19] I didn't get to write the script. If I did, then I would have made that part of my story different. God wrote it. He taught me over many years, and with great patience for my stubbornness, to accept my story, the bad and the good. I can do that because I love and trust the author.

Chapter Thirteen

THE LOSS

When I lost someone I loved dearly…

There was a season when I experienced back-to-back negative events in my life for two years. Not catastrophic ones but daily ones, mean little punches on the regular, little foxes that snuck in day after day to destroy the vineyard. I remembered asking God when I would finally catch a break. *God, can I have something good happen to balance out this steady river of bad things, these problems?* Yet the balance never came. My joy as a saved person gradually dimmed. It became harder for me to find it. It became a chore to rediscover it, to re-ignite it. The praise songs about God's love that used to lift me up could barely raise my eyes, let alone my hands. I started to believe that I was the exception, the only one again, like Elijah. Those songs didn't refer to me. God's love was for everyone else but me. It felt like His love was divided eight billion ways, and there wasn't enough left over for me.

I started putting myself on trial. What am I doing that's so wrong in God's eyes? What is the crime that I'm being punished for? Did I marry the wrong person because it all seemed to happen after I got remarried? Did that choice make me fall out of line with God's will for my life and so I fell out of favor? It was like He took His presence away. I couldn't find Him even when I prayed.

Then the catastrophe came, what felt like the final blow. Let me explain with some backstory.

My Golden Retriever's name was Bruce Wayne. His demeanor was nothing like his namesake's. This Bruce Wayne (Brucey, Bubby, or Big Juicy... he answered to all of those) was like sunshine – bright, warm, and joyful. He brought a smile to the faces of everyone who met him.

Soon after he turned six years old, Brucey started acting sluggish at the end of our long walks. I thought it was just that he was hot and tired. It was August in Florida after all, probably the most brutal month for heat and humidity. Then one day he didn't finish his food, and the next day he wouldn't even come to the bowl when I filled it. This was a guy who came running at the sound of kibble hitting his bowl. His breath had a funky smell, not that he ever had the freshest breath, and he stopped greeting me at the door when I came home. The following day, I took him to the vet, thinking he maybe had a tooth infection.

They did an exam and ran some tests and found signs of a mass in his spleen. Though there was hope that it could be benign and treatable in some way, he was at risk for his spleen rupturing. I cancelled all my appointments for the next day, including one for a tire change. I'd found a nail in my tire the day before I took him to the vet. I drove with my nail-in-the-tire to the emergency vet's office. This was during the COVID19 pandemic so I wasn't allowed inside. I sat and cried in my car for four hours while they did more testing on him. I okayed the $9,000 charge on my credit card for a splenectomy. I would have found a way to pay it off gradually. After all, he was like my kid. If the mass had been benign, the surgery would have been curative. I prayed for it to be benign. The receptionist came out and brought me tissues, and after taking in my red, puffy face, she told me to just keep the whole box.

I received the call that it was definitely malignant and had already metastasized to his liver, and there were micro-metastases to his heart and lungs. Any of these metastases could rupture, which would cause him to bleed internally either around his heart or into his abdomen. If the bleeds were large, he would die immediately. If they were small, he would die more slowly and agonizingly. There was no point in putting him through the splenectomy since it wouldn't improve his prognosis. They recommended a biopsy to find out which malignant cancer it was.

It was the worst kind, rare and uncommon for his breed, disseminated histiocytic sarcoma, and they suspected he had the worst phenotype of an already terrible, inevitably fatal disease. It had already spread. There was chemo available that most dogs tolerated well, but it wasn't likely to cure him, just give him time.

Goldens usually live ten to twelve years when they're healthy, sometimes longer, and he was only six. My Brucey was healthy, until he wasn't. I thought we were only halfway through our life journey together. As the vet updated me, she assured me that he was in the back with them, loving all their attention and socializing with them.

That was my dog, you see, and anyone who has loved a Golden can attest to the breed's nature. It made his day to meet people. When I walked him, if he saw someone about to pass him, he would perk up, do a prance and grin wide. I never trained him to love everyone he met. He just did. Whatever the most precious material is in heaven, that was what my dog's heart was made of. He loved unconditionally.

He loved me unconditionally.

My husband told me my boy had a heart like God wanted us to have. He was joyful every day, consistently, from the time he got up to when he laid down to sleep. He was the same way all the time. He welcomed everyone to his home. He never growled at anyone or any other dog. He rarely barked and only at one of his family members, usually me, to either let him out to potty or to feed him or to get up and play with him. Other dogs would bark at him and often lunge at him. He never barked back but would wag his tail, look at the dog, then look back at me as if to question, "What's their deal?"

Whenever he saw another human while we were on our walks, it was as if he had this expectancy to meet them. He would wait until we were near them, and then prance and grin and wag his tail like he was trying to reassure them that even though he was big, he was friendly and harmless. He desperately wanted them to pet him and call him a good boy. Even if they were across the street, he'd sit facing them, with perfect posture, looking as handsome as can be, waiting for them to welcome him over to meet them. He noticed everyone. He treated everyone the same, like a friend.

The only exception was his family. He loved us extra, especially my sons. He was my youngest son's best friend. I was his momma, his person. He adored me; it was in his eyes as he followed me around, making sure he could always see me. He was a momma's boy. I was so loved by this beautiful, gentle soul, and the idea of losing that love, a love that stayed with me when everyone else left, put a grief in me that pierced through and through. I felt like I was being robbed, like love was being taken from me, stolen, harshly and wrongfully.

I thought I had time, but I didn't. I thought I would see him grow older gradually, but I didn't.

I've lived my life scared to make mistakes and to have to live with the disappointment from those mistakes, mainly in myself. I was filled with regret for the times I left him alone too long. I knew I made mistakes with my dog, but if he could have spoken, if you could have asked him to tell you what those mistakes were, he would have had nothing to say. He never held me to my mistakes.

He would stay facing the door after I left for work, waiting for me to come home. I scheduled my day around him. Everyone at my office knew I went home during my lunch break to let my dog out and give him a treat.

I raised him from when he was an eight-week-old puppy. He stayed puppy-size for about five minutes. Both my children were particular in their eating, so when I finally had a kid who was a good eater, I overfed him. He grew to be a solid one hundred pounds. Once when I was walking him in our neighborhood, someone asked me if I put a leash on him or a saddle. A lot of people mistook him for being a female. *He's just a very pretty boy*, I would say. His brown eyes were expressive, like human eyes. It was heartbreaking to see them when he got sick. They became downcast and tired. He had upbeat moments, but they wore him out. He wouldn't even lift his head to sniff the cat's butt when she passed by, and I think she felt a little dejected by that.

I wrote this chapter longhand in my personal journal, never intending for it to be read by anyone. When I wrote it, I'd been crying for days. My eyes were pink and puffy, my nose crimson and swollen. The upper half of my face hurt. My cheeks were raw from wiping tears.

I was under the broom tree, not curled up in a ball like I wanted to be, but flat on my face, actively pleading and asking God for relief, for a miracle, a testimony. Surely I couldn't sacrifice any more tears at the altar than I'd already shed. I was already down from one bad thing after another. *Please don't make me live without him, this bright ray of sunlight in my life,* I begged Jesus. I didn't know how to live without him. So I asked the miracle-worker to heal him completely. I asked the way-maker to tell me what to do. I was a decisive person, but I had no idea what to do next.

I'll share with you some of the things I saw and learned, as I laid prostate and unable to help either the one I loved or myself. I sensed God was there with me. Somehow, I kept breathing and my heart kept pumping, though at times I wondered how it didn't break apart into pieces.

I saw a side of my husband that I'd never witnessed before. We had been going through a rough patch, the kind where you want to give up, but there's that covenant with God you have to uphold, so that's the only reason why you're staying. I saw that man cry for the first time. He drove an hour and a half to come hold me, love on our dog, and to comfort me, and two hours later, he had to drive back another hour and a half to see his next client. I didn't know he loved the dog that much. My husband had a dopey voice he used to narrate for Brucey. We were going to make an Instagram account for him with my husband doing a voiceover in the videos. Seeing my husband lay down next to Brucey and tell him what a good boy he was and how much he was loved, broke a pride in me. It crumbled resentment. Love shone through. It flooded through.

I heard my Heavenly Father whisper to my aching spirit, "You need to remember to love. Love the ones I've given you in your life, and when you think you've loved them enough, then love them even more and love them harder." God needed to soften my heart. The experience didn't just soften it but turned it into mush. Before my dog, I'd never had someone close to me die or get so sick that they had only days to live. I'd never felt that crushing despair before. My grandparents lived in India while I grew up in America, and I hardly knew them. My parents were still living and so were the aunts and uncles that I knew well.

I asked my husband if God was punishing me for something I'd done wrong. Brucey's illness hit me the hardest, so surely I'd done something wrong, and my beautiful boy was suffering for it. He said, "God loves us like we are His own children. Would you punish one of your sons by killing something he loved like how you love Brucey? You wouldn't even consider it."

God loves me better than I love my own children and better than I loved my Brucey. He was and still is right here with me. He's with me under the tree that I both curse and bless. I may never understand what's happening on this side of heaven, but He already knew what was coming. He hadn't left me alone for any of it, and whatever outcome awaited me, whatever lay ahead, He was already there in the midst of it, in the mess of it, ready to catch me at the end of it.

I prayed for a miracle, for God to heal him of cancer. I prayed that I would crawl out from under the broom tree with a miracle story of God's healing ability with my bouncing, beautiful boy by my side.

You think you have time, but you don't.

You don't realize how precious some moments are until they become memories.

You think you have years with the one you love, but then you only have days.

How would you live those days if they were all you had left?

Some people may think, *it's a dog, not a person.* There are some dogs we love like people. They become family members. Brucey was our family. My dad called him our Gentle Giant. To know him was to love him, even if you weren't particularly fond of dogs.

I moved into my home May of 2014. It was the first home I bought after my divorce. I got my first dog as an eight-week-old puppy that August. He was part of the house. He made it a home for us, full of love, playfulness, and lightheartedness. He was a constant part of my life. I never thought about living without him there.

I didn't know how to live in the house without him. I pleaded with God. *How am I supposed to be here day after day without him?* My kids were only there half the week since I was timesharing with their dad. My husband and I maintained two households in separate cities about an hour and a half apart because of his timesharing agreement with his ex-wife. My parents were living in India. Brucey was my constant companion. He was the kid who stayed every day and followed me around. He got up when I got up, slept when I slept, and he sometimes would drink his water when he saw me drinking water. On the days that my kids left to be with their dad, this was the kid that I hugged and fussed over.

"I can't live without him," I whispered to God, "Please don't make me. I'm always saying goodbye. To my kids, my husband. Don't make me say goodbye forever to my dog. He's my boy too."

God answered back to my heart, "You're thinking you will be all alone and that your home will be empty without him, but where can you go and where can you live, that I am not there with you? Open your mind to receive that truth. I've said it so many ways in My Word."

"He will not leave you nor forsake you" (Deuteronomy 31:6, NKJV).

"God is not man, that He should lie, Nor a son of man, that He should repent. Has he said, and will He not do? Or has He spoken, and will He not make it good?" (Numbers 23:19, NKJV).

"Behold I am with you and will keep you wherever you go… I will not leave you…" (Genesis 28:15, NKJV).

"For He Himself has said, 'I will never leave you nor forsake you'" (Hebrews 13:5, NKJV).

"The Lord is near to those who have a broken heart, And saves such as have a contrite spirit" (Psalms 34:18, NKJV).

As I searched these verses and sought out His promise in them, I felt them comfort my raw wounded heart. Whenever I felt the hurt, I would refer to them.

Now there are some sad people who believe that there can be no animals in heaven. I've heard people say that our pets won't be there because we won't have the same desires in heaven that we have here on earth. So why are there mansions in heaven? "In My Father's house are many mansions; if it were not so, I would have told you," Jesus says in John 14:2 (NKJV). Why would we desire housing there? For rooms to sleep in, bathrooms to use?

I've heard arguments that there is no mention of animals in heaven in the Bible. During the time the Bible was written, I don't think people loved domesticated animals like family but there is mention of horses. "Now I saw heaven opened, and behold, a white horse. And He who sat on him was called Faithful and True, and in righteousness He judges and makes war… And the armies of heaven, clothed in fine linen, white and clean, followed Him on white horses" (Revelation 19:11-14, NKJV). In heaven, why will we want to see the people we knew and loved here who passed on? Why would we have that desire? Who will they be to us in heaven?

I don't believe every single living creature will be in heaven. I think we get our answer when we pray about it specifically. It's the relationship of the believer that makes the difference. Billy Graham said, "God will prepare everything for our perfect happiness in heaven, and if it takes my dog being there, I believe he'll be there." [20] God was with me through every step of my dog's illness, and I sought His voice. Not once did He convict me that my dog, whom I loved like my own child, wouldn't be there.

I wrote the following on October 2, 2020:

"Today is the last day I get up early to let my boy out and feed him breakfast. The past few days have been chicken for breakfast, steak for dinner and a whole lot of forbidden, canine-obesity-promoting treats in-between. On September 22nd, the day after my younger

149

son's birthday, my boy took a turn for the worse. It was a steady decline with no remission. He seemed better after the first dose of chemo treatment, so we were encouraged that he was responding to the therapy. He should have continued to improve after the second chemo treatment, but the opposite happened.

"His abdomen started getting more distended, his hind feet swelled with pitting edema, and we watched him struggle with every movement, especially trying to stand up. His urine turned a dark orange color, and he had to go less frequently. He was bleeding into his urine. His organs were failing. The oncology vet confirmed that his red blood cell count had dropped dramatically so his anemia had worsened. This explained the weakness and fatigue we saw in him. His liver had enlarged and an ultrasound revealed that all the cavitations, which represented the tumors, were all still there and had possibly increased in size from the previous scan. It was what I had feared.

"My hopes that had slowly, cautiously built up after the first chemo treatment were crushed. I cried out to God whenever I could, meaning when I wasn't doing my daily duties and house-running chores. Usually there is so much to be done that there are only rare, infrequent times you are allotted to utterly lose your composure, and I think every mother knows what I mean by that.

"*Why was it my boy*, I cried out from under the broom tree? *Let me go with him*, I begged. I started rationalizing that my sons would be okay without me, that their dad could raise them. This was the irrational madness of grief. My logical mind knew my sons needed me and loved me as desperately and completely as I them.

"No, I would live on with this piece of my heart permanently missing, with this pain. When you lose a family member you love, no one can replace them. There's little solace in the fact that you have others.

"Why did he get better after the first chemo treatment then? Was God just being extra cruel? Was He being sadistic and giving me hope only to snatch it away? And then I remembered my husband and I kneeling together in prayer beside Brucey, asking God for a miracle of complete healing. But we also asked that if it wasn't possible, if it wasn't in His will, we pleaded for more time. My son's birthday was coming up, and he was Brucey's best friend. I've collected so many precious memories over the years of them cuddling and laying on the floor together. My son would boop his nose and tell him he was such a good boy, a funny boy, and that he loved him oh so very much. We didn't want Brucey to pass before his best friend's birthday.

"Friends, sometimes the miracle is not in a complete healing. It's in precious God-given time. The time that this fallen world with its sickness and disease would have robbed you of is something only God can restore. My boy was playing and wagging his tail at his best friend's birthday party when he should have only had a few days left from his moment of diagnosis. And that gift of time, seeing him like his old playful self, was a miracle in and of itself.

"It's October 2nd, the last day I'll do a lot of things for my boy, things that I scheduled my day around, because I'd raised him like he was my own child. As every minute passes towards the time when the vet will come to our home to administer the medication to put him to sleep, I feel like I'm being pressed down. I feel crushed under the branches of this ordinary tree. I don't know how to say goodbye to him, Jesus.

"My boy is lying beside me enjoying some outside time by the pool. I feel regret, and I tell God that I should have let him swim in the pool more often. And my loving Father speaks to my heart, "He's going to swim all he wants.'"

"I took precious care of my boy the best I could, like he was my own flesh-and-blood child. I'm going to hold him and tell him I love him when he closes his soulful brown eyes for the last time and takes his last breath. It's all I can do for him at the end. And Jesus has whispered to my heart that it's enough and to just leave the rest to Him.

"Jesus is the one who will take over from there. In fact, He is with us now as we spend a few precious hours together by the pool, as I write on these tear-stained pages. My Savior is here. My best friend is here. And He will be there to greet my sweet boy on the other side. I don't know how anyone goes through this without the love of Jesus Christ. I certainly don't have that kind of strength in myself.

"Galatians 2:20 (KJV) says, 'I am crucified with Christ: nevertheless I live; yet not I, but Christ liveth in me: and the life which I now live in the flesh I live by the faith of the Son of God, who loved me, and gave himself for me.'

"Today is the day my baby boy, my golden beautiful boy, dies, but it is also the day he goes to heaven. I believe that with all my heart. A love this pure and loyal can only come from God, our good and loving Father. Jesus died for me and allowed me to have a relationship and connection to God, and it is through that assurance I know I will see my boy again one day. I will see him whole, restored, and happy, and I will be too.

"He's going to be rolling in the greenest grass and running and jumping like he did before he became ill. He'll be completely restored and without any more pain in his body. He's going to greet me at those gates one day like he did every day he was here with me, with a wagging tail and all the love in the world contained in a pair of amber-brown eyes.

"I know there is a peace and restoration for me on the other side of this. Though I feel like I'm crumbling under the weight of a mountain of grief, God is sustaining me. He is encouraging me through the words of friends who have experienced this kind of loss too. The comfort I've received in these days is something I can't say enough 'thank yous' for. Just like Elijah, my God will hold me here until I can get up and push forward again.

"If I had known what was going to happen six years ago, sitting on the breeder's floor surrounded by him and his littermates, tiny fluffy balls of yellow-gold fur trying to nibble my toes, I would have still picked him. I would have chosen him again and again. He was the biggest one of his batch, and instead of biting at my feet he clumsily walked over to me wagging his tail and laid his head on my leg. He still likes to lay his head on my leg.

"I imagine there are a lot of man's (and woman's) best friends in heaven waiting to be united. I once saw a picture online of a group of golden retrievers lined up at a gate, and the caption read, "This is what I imagine the entrance to heaven looking like."

"In case it is like that, and one day you reach those gates before I do, look for the golden that is bigger than most and unusually docile, even for his breed. His mom overfed him when he was a puppy, and he was the largest of his litter. He'll probably have a tennis ball in his mouth that he's insistent you take out. He will want you to reach inside his mouth past those big teeth to grab hold of it. Don't be afraid to do just that. He'd never bite. He's the kindest, gentlest dog. Take that ball and toss it into the air for him. He loves that. Do it for me, until I can get there to toss it myself."

AΩ

Even in his last hour, he was wagging his tail and trying to greet the vet who came to our home to administer the euthanasia. He chose his spot on our living room floor, where he had chewed on his favorite toys, where he had cuddled with his best friend. He chose his new favorite toy, a stuffed bunny that I'd bought for him that week, and he waited for us to join him there for the last minutes of his life.

I knew that at any moment God could have healed him if it had been His will to do so. I trusted that He would explain it all to me when I got to heaven one day. It's because of the sacrifice that Jesus made on the cross that I had a connection and relationship with an Almighty God, that I had the comforting presence of the Holy Spirit, so my dog, who was like my child, could go to the evergreen pastures of heaven. It was because of Jesus that I would see him again and hold him once more. So much pain in this fragile human heart and just a tiny hope in the flaming face of agony, but it was enough, just enough hope, to survive one of the worst days of my life.

I wrote the following after my baby died:

"There are moments in life that utterly destroy you. Your heart squeezes so hard that you wonder about the contraction it's still able to make afterwards, that it's capable of the next beat and that it didn't disintegrate

155

under the pressure. There are moments where your breath catches in your chest, and you marvel at its ability to expand again for another inspiration after such a blow.

"These are my best attempts to describe such moments, and I still feel that my words don't do them justice. One such moment for me was when I saw my sons' names on my finalized divorce documents. The finalization of their family's death with their full names and birthdates spelled out like the casualties of a murder. Another moment was when I heard Brucey take his last breath, when the life left his body. A body that was once full of energy, able to run at full speed and jump with enthusiasm, in a moment, was limp and lifeless. His abdomen bloated and riddled with a cancer that I wished had a face so I could punch it in its teeth and knock it flat out. These are seconds of time that shake you, and you are changed irrevocably by them. The reflection you see the next time you glance in a mirror is altered, maybe not so obviously to others on the outside, but a stranger looks back at you. You may be the only one who realizes what lies haunted behind your eyes.

"It's unhealthy to ignore grief or bottle it up, to try compartmentalizing the pain, and attempt to bury it. Go to a quiet place and be still before God. Let the grief pierce you. Let the tears flow. Cry out to God and tell Him you are angry or upset or just done and over it. He can take it. He wants to take it.

"Under the broom tree is where I crawl, and it's where I have learned to survive. I don't plan for the future there. It's where I get through the next few hours, the next few minutes. I eat enough food and drink enough water to survive. And God always meets me there.

"The most important thing I can do there in the storms of life is praise Him. It seems counterintuitive and like the last thing I would want to do.

"But it's critical.

"God, the Heavenly Father, Creator of the universe, Alpha and Omega, is enthroned in heaven and angelic beings surround Him with praise that is without ceasing. But His gaze is down here, on us, His beloved, fallen, image-bearing creation. He's looking intently for a shout of praise, a hallelujah, a hosanna, from us. And when you offer that praise from a place of pain and despair, from the cracked ravines of a broken heart, my friend, even the angels are awestruck.

"He is still good, even when life utterly sucks, even when you don't want to get out of bed in the morning because it would require you to face life as it is, and it's not at all what you want it to be. When you don't want to wake up to an empty house that is too quiet, He is there. When there is no sweet face and loving eyes to greet you, God is there.

"So don't hold back your pain and your praise. You are in powerful company. Job says, 'Though he slay me, yet will I trust Him' (Job 13:15, NKJV). And Jesus

Himself proclaims on His knees in Gethsemane's garden, '... nevertheless, not as I will, but as You will' (Matthew 26:39, NKJV).

"With them, we can bow our heads to His will.

"From under the broom tree, I shouted at Him, 'God, You are still good. Even though I hate this, and I'm so angry, and I don't understand at all, I love You.'

"When I was experiencing negative life events daily over the course of a few years, I was letting my faith, my trust in God, die in increments. With each disappointment and with each stress and negative life event, I had no control. I would throw my hands up in exasperation. The death of my beloved family member was like the final hit. It also woke me up to what I had allowed to happen in my mind. I'd let my trust in God dissolve. My boy's death made me throw my hands up in completely undone surrender.

"It was only sometime after that I realized the change He was creating in me, the transforming of my character. I started to notice how much I had rushed, how I would get impatient, how I would be quick to judge on what seemed like little things. I began to realize I had no right. I felt the humbling. I recognized it and acknowledged it and said okay to it. God, You are in charge, not me. Whatever negative thing happens next, You will either walk me through it or carry me. And it might get really bad. He knocked me down to my foundations so He could slowly build me back up, fashioning my character for what would come next in my life.

"God owes me nothing.

I owe Him everything."

Chapter Fourteen

BACK TO THE ORDINARY MAN AND HIS TREE

Remember when I said God wasn't done helping Elijah recover after he got up from under the broom tree?

"... and he went in the strength of that food forty days and forty nights as far as Horeb, the mountain of God" (1 Kings 19:8, NKJV). That verse makes me think of *lembas* bread from *The Lord of the Rings*. In the story, *lembas* was an elvish waybread that could sustain a man for days, which made it useful for a long journey. The bread that Elijah consumed when under the broom tree had supernatural quality. If he started roughly around Beersheeba, then he traveled on foot just over 300 miles to Mount Horeb.

Mount Horeb is another name for Mount Sinai, which is where Moses was given the Ten Commandments. It's where God revealed His law to His people. For Elijah, it also became a place of revelation. Once he got there, he stayed in a cave, and God chose that time to lovingly confront him and address his spiritual need.

"And there he went into a cave, and spent the night in that place; and behold, the word of the Lord came to him, and He said to him, 'What are you doing here, Elijah?' So he said, 'I have been very zealous for the Lord God of hosts; for the children of Israel have forsaken Your covenant, torn down Your altars, and killed Your prophets with the sword. I alone am left; and they seek to take my life'" (1 Kings 19:9-10, NKJV).

What are you doing here, Elijah?

Elijah wasn't ready for this conversation with God when he was under the broom tree, and God knew it. God's timing often makes no sense to us, but He's never wrong. He knows when to give the revelation that will set you free. Author Barb Roose said, "God is your future. He is your outcome. God knows our storyline from the beginning to the middle and the end. You can be certain He knows how to land the plane when the time comes." [21]

God sees through to the heart of every man and woman. He knew Elijah was bottling up his thoughts. God gave him food, rest, and solitude, but now it was time to dig up the buried pain.

"Then He said, 'Go out, and stand on the mountain before the Lord.' And behold, the Lord passed by, and a great and strong wind tore into the mountains and broke the rocks in pieces before the Lord, but the Lord was not in the wind; and after the wind an earthquake, but the Lord was not in the earthquake; and after the earthquake a fire, but the Lord was not in the fire…" (1 Kings 19:11-12, NKJV).

Elijah witnessed one roaring, boisterous natural event after another but that's not where God was. You need quiet to listen for His voice; it's something you have to be attuned to. You need to be without any interferences or intrusions to hear Him.

Why?

"…and after the fire a still small voice" (1Kings 19:12, NKJV).

That's where God was and still is. Closer than the air you breathe. Near to you. Sure His voice can thunder (Psalm 18:13) and can sound like "many waters" (Ezekiel 43:2 and Revelation 1:15), and it can have "the sound of a trumpet" (Revelation 1:10 and Revelation 4:1), but when you need to hear from Him, it's in the quiet, away from the distractions and the noise.

Elijah recognized God's voice. "So it was, when Elijah heard it, that he wrapped his face in his mantle and went out and stood at the entrance of the cave. Suddenly a voice came to him, and said, 'What are you doing here, Elijah?'" (1 Kings 19:13, NKJV). God asked him the same question as before.

And Elijah, stuck in his feelings, replied the same way. "And he said, 'I have been very zealous for the Lord God of hosts; because the children of Israel have forsaken Your covenant, torn down Your altars, and killed your prophets with the sword. I alone am left; and they seek to take my life'" (1 Kings 19:14, NKJV).

Elijah had expectations of himself, and he was falling short in his own eyes. God didn't create this expectation of him; Elijah did. Where had Elijah failed? I suspect it was in his mind. Ambition is a double-edged sword, as is perfectionism. Both can teeter into unhealthy anxiety. According to Kevin Halloran, Charles Spurgeon said, "Anxiety does not empty tomorrow of its sorrows, but only empties today of its strength."[22] Maybe Elijah expected Jezebel and Ahab to leave him alone, to finally show him some respect. He had followed through on all he'd said, but Jezebel was still after him.

I heard a message from Pastor Steven Furtick where he pointed out that verses 10 and 14 were the exact same verses. Pastor said that Elijah had rehearsed this sad story in his head so many times, for forty days and forty nights. If the enemy can get you to rehearse the wrong story enough, it will be the only story you have by the time you get to the cave. He pointed out that you can have Jesus in your heart and Jezebel in your head.[23]

Elijah was feeling sorry for himself, wallowing in it. He knew he was in God's presence but gave the same answer. R. T. Kendall in his book, *These Are The Days of*

Elijah: How God Uses Ordinary People to Do Extraordinary Things, said, "Self-righteousness is feeling we deserve the credit. Self-pity, the twin of self-righteousness, often comes from feeling we are not getting noticed, not getting the credit."[24]

Elijah said he was the only one left when he spoke to the Israelites on Mount Carmel. He spoke incorrectly at the most pivotal miracle of his career, and God still worked His miracle through him. Elijah didn't get it all right every time. Just like us, he slipped up. You don't have to be perfect for God to use you. Mark Batterson said, "God doesn't call the qualified, He qualifies the called."[25]

Mount Carmel was the highlight event of Elijah's career. If his life were a movie reel, that scene was the climax of the film but it didn't mean God was done with him. God answered Elijah without calling him out on his error. "Then the Lord said to him: 'Go, return on your way to the Wilderness of Damascus; and when you arrive, anoint Hazael as king over Syria. Also you shall anoint Jehu the son of Nimshi as king over Israel. And Elisha the son of Shaphat of Abel Meholah you shall anoint as prophet in your place. It shall be that whoever escapes the sword of Hazael, Jehu will kill; and whoever escapes the sword of Jehu, Elisha will kill. Yet I have reserved seven thousand in Israel, all whose knees have not bowed to Baal, and every mouth that has not kissed him'" (1 Kings 19:15-18, NKJV).

God had already solved it; He had worked out Elijah's future. He sent that man back the same way he had come. I haven't seen anxiety improve by simply avoiding the trigger. Usually, avoidance worsens the anxiety, or at least allows it to persist. God made him face his fear and He let Elijah know gently, not in any disdainful or condescending way, that he was not alone and that he was not the only one left. God still had a purpose for him.

Later, He even sent Elijah back in front of Ahab and Jezebel to confront them about yet another abhorrent sin they had committed – the false accusation and murder of an innocent man named Naboth – and Elijah informed the wicked couple how they would both die violent deaths. To Ahab, he announces, "…'This is what the Lord says: In the place where dogs licked up Naboth's blood, dogs will lick up your blood – yes, yours!'" (1 Kings 21:19, NIV).

"And also concerning Jezebel the Lord says: 'Dogs will devour Jezebel by the wall of Jezreel'" (1 Kings 21:23, NIV). And later we read, "But when they went out to bury her, they found nothing except her skull, feet and her hands. They went back and told Jehu, who said, 'This is the word of the Lord that He spoke through His servant Elijah the Tishbite: On the plot of ground at Jezreel dogs will devour Jezebel's flesh. Jezebel's body will be like dung on the ground in the plot at Jezreel, so no that no one will be able to say, 'This is Jezebel'"" (2 Kings 9:35-37, NIV).

Jezebel never killed Elijah like she swore she would. God saw to it that she never got her filthy hands on him. In fact, Elijah didn't die. As he was walking with his successor Elisha, "... suddenly a chariot of fire and horses of fire appeared and separated the two of them, and Elijah went up to heaven in a whirlwind" (2 Kings 2:11, NIV).

J.C. Ryle said, "The best of men are only men at their very best. Patriarchs, prophets, and apostles, martyrs, fathers, reformers, puritans -- all are sinners, who need a Savior: holy, useful, honorable in their place – but sinners all." [26] What did Elijah find under that broom tree? When he was hungry, God fed him. When he needed to be still and take rest, God protectively, like any good father, took him under His mighty wing and watched over him until he was ready to get up again. In the same way, whatever brings you to your knees, to the end of yourself, to the broom tree, know God will meet you there. He's more than able to provide what you need to rise up, start over, and breathe the free air.

We are our worst masters. God hasn't cursed you because you have anxiety or depression; you're not less blessed by Him because of these. Know when to surrender it. Know when to sit under the broom tree and lay down every ounce of pride, every bit of ego, all of your self-sufficiency, and put aside whatever education you've acquired, and whatever emotional intelligence you believe you have. If you've ever suffered from anxiety or depression, if either or both ever paralyzed you, if you've ever come to the point in your own mind where you wished your life were over because it was too hard to live, then know that you are in good company -- with one of the greatest prophets to walk the earth. God didn't try to change Elijah's personality and miraculously make him un-depressed and un-anxious. He took him as he was, fully seeing his crippling fear and his fiery zeal. It's as if God said, "I'll take both. I love both."

God didn't spare His own Son. Knowing He would suffer a horrific death, Jesus still asked, "'Father, if You are willing, take this cup from me; yet not my will, but Yours be done.' An angel from heaven appeared to him and strengthened him. And being in anguish, he prayed more earnestly, and his sweat was like drops of blood falling to the ground" (Luke 22:42-44, NIV).

What are you doing here, _____?

Put your name in the blank space. When you come to the end of your strength, find some solitude, and you'll hear God ask this question with your name at the end of it. Answer with honesty like Elijah did. God's not done with you, even when you're done with yourself. If you wake up tomorrow with a heartbeat and breath in your lungs, keep going, because God still has plans and purpose for you.

REFERENCES

1. Halley, Henry H. (2000). "The Old Testament," The Monarchy: David, Solomon, and the Divided Kingdom. Deluxe Edition, Zondervan. (p 224-232)

2. Peretti, F. (2000). *No More Bullies: For Those Who Wound or Are Wounded.* Thomas Nelson. (p 179)

3. Graham, Billy. Interview. Conducted by Greta Van Susteran. 2010.

4. Furtick, Steven @stevenfurtick. "God can't bless who you pretend to be." March 8, 2017, 8:58pm.

5. Warren, R. (2002). *The Purpose Driven Life: What on Earth Am I Here For?.* Zondervan. (p 148)

6. Gruver, Diana. "Charles Spurgeon Knew It Was Possible to Be Faithful and Depressed." *Christianity Today*, 26 Feb 2021, https://www.christianitytoday.com/ct/2021/february-web-only/diana-gruver-companions-darkness-spurgeon-depression.html

7. Brencher, Hannah (@hannahbrencher). May 13, 2022. https://www.instagram.com/hannahbrencher/?hl=en

8. Batterson, Mark. You Version Bible App. "Whisper: How To Hear the Voice of God, 5-Day Reading Plan from Mark Batterson." https://www.bible.com/reading-plans/8721-whisper-how-hear-the-voice-of-god-mark-batterson/day/5

9. Wilkerson, Jr., Rich. "Work Your Weakness," Elevation Church. Feb 20, 2022. North Carolina. Sermon.

10. O'Toole, Garson. "The Greatest Trick the Devil Ever Pulled Was Convincing the World He Didn't Exist." *Quote Investigator.* March 20, 2018. https://quoteinvestigator.com/2018/03/20/devil/?amp=1

11. Holmes, Phillip. "Drunk In Love: The Danger of Infatuation in Dating." desiringGod.org

12. Jaynes, Sharon. "When You Feel Discouraged." *Girlfriends in God*, 11 Nov 2022, https://girlfriendsingod.com/when-you-feel-discouraged-3/

13. "Soren Kierkegaard Quotes." *Quotes.net.* STANDS4 LLC, 2023. Web. 30 Jan 2023. https://www.quotes.net/quote/49962>.

14. Furtick, Steven @stevenfurtick. "God cannot heal what you hide (See Proverbs 28:13)." Dec 18, 2017, 4:53pm.

15. Jaynes, Sharon. "Sometimes Healing Takes Time." *Girlfriends in God*, 11 Feb 2021,

https://girlfriendsingod.com/sometimes-healing-takes-time/

16. Williamson, Marianne. Quoted in article from The Bee Hive. "How Can I Forgive Them." *The Bee Hive.* 22 Oct 2022, https://www.thebeehive.live/blog/tag/What+does+unforgiveness+look+like%3F

17. Shirer, P. (2015). *Fervent.* B&H Publishing Group.

18. Batterson, Mark @MarkBatterson. "the circumstances we ask God to change are often the circumstances God is using to change us @MaxLucado @NCC." Sept 8, 2013, 11:13am.

19. Winkler, Erica. "What The Bible Says Freedom Actually Looks Like." *Relevant Magazine,* 24 July 2018, https://relevantmagazine.com/faith/what-does-freedom-mean/

20. Graham, Billy. Quoted by Jim Daly with Paul Batura. "Do Pets Go To Heaven?." Focus on The Family. 9 Nov 2010, https://jimdaly.focusonthefamily.com/do-pets-go-to-heaven/

21. Roose, B. (2021). *Surrendered: 40 Devotions to Help You Let Go and Live Like Jesus.* Abingdom Press. (p 38)

22. Hollaran, Kevin. "40 Charles Spurgeon Quotes on Anxiety, Fear, and Worry." *Anchored In Christ.* 29 May 2021, https://www.kevinhalloran.net/40-charles-spurgeon-quotes-on-anxiety-fear-and-worry/#google_vignette

23. Furtick, Steven. "God's Got Your Back Part 2," September 11, 2022. Elevation Church. North Carolina. Sermon.

24. Kendall, R.T. (2013). *These Are The Days of Elijah: How God Uses Ordinary People to Do Extraordinary Things*. Chosen Books. (p 137)

25. Batterson, Mark @MarkBatterson. "God doesn't call the QUALIFIED. He qualifies the CALLED." Mar 16, 2015, 7:53am.

26. Ryle, J. C. Posted by *The J. C. Ryle Archive* on Jan 12, 2018, 6:34am. https://www.jcryle.info/2018/01/the-best-of-men-are-men-at-best.html

About
Kharis Publishing:

Kharis Publishing, an imprint of Kharis Media LLC, is a leading Christian and inspirational book publisher based in Aurora, Chicago metropolitan area, Illinois. Kharis' dual mission is to give voice to under-represented writers (including women and first-time authors) and equip orphans in developing countries with literacy tools. That is why, for each book sold, the publisher channels some of the proceeds into providing books and computers for orphanages in developing countries so that these kids may learn to read, dream, and grow. For a limited time, Kharis Publishing is accepting unsolicited queries for nonfiction (Christian, self-help, memoirs, business, health and wellness) from qualified leaders, professionals, pastors, and ministers. Learn more at: https://kharispublishing.com/

CPSIA information can be obtained
at www.ICGtesting.com
Printed in the USA
JSHW010931250623
43581JS00005B/22

9 781637 462126